Clara Janés

To Keep the House and Shut One's Mouth: Of Women and Literature

Translation & Notes

Anne Pasero

- STOCKCERO -

1st. Stockcero edition: 2021

ISBN: 978-1-949938-07-4
Library of Congress Control Number: 2021940221

Set in Linotype Granjon font family typeface
Printed in the United States of America on acid-free paper.

Published by Stockcero, Inc.
3785 N.W. 82nd Avenue
Doral, FL 33166
USA
stockcero@stockcero.com

www.stockcero.com

Clara Janés

To Keep the House and Shut One's Mouth: Of Women and Literature

Translation & Notes

Anne Pasero

Translator's note:
All of the translations into English are done by me, with permission of the author.

Contents

I- The Prism 11
Bibliography 17

II- Priestesses, Courtesans, Princesses and Women in Love: Paradoxical Writing....................19
Sexualized Writing 20
Clamor In The Temple 21
With A Fish In The Chest....................24
I Will Climb Up the Erect Palm Tree 27
The Ingenuous Song 30
Norms For Women's Rooms 32
Subtlety and Impulse 35
Korean Courtesan Women....................40
To Say And To Tell 43
Murasaki....................47
The One Hundred Nights 50
Bibliography 53

III- With The Harmonious From The Sea: 57
Woman and Writing in Greece and Rome 57
Islands And Fragments 58
Untamed Hair and The Triumphant Ribbon....................63
The Freedom of Water 68
A Light Beyond....................72
Rome, a Circle In a Square....................75
Bibliography 85

IV- Closed Gardens; Open Pleasures: Arab-Andalusian Women Poets....................87

Caravan Of Stories 89
The Body As A Goal 93
Missives and Wrongs 96
Safe From Thirst 100
Persistence Of The Aroma 106
Bibliography 109

V- Love From Afar And Body To Body 111
Women Troubadours, Warriors and Enlightened Ones 111
The Shadow Of Plato 114
To Sing What One Might Not Want 118
To Take A Husband Or Remain A Maiden 123
Shouts And Laughter 127
The Soul Or The Imagination 131
Inferno Of Love 135
Sacred Furor 140
The Archetype 148
Bibliography 153

VI- That Time In Which Queens Were Slaves Or The Disguise....157
Intimate Prisons 158
Blame And Virtue 162
Dressed Up And Covered Up 166
Crows Of The Convents 171
Under The Volcano 177
Incestuous Mask 185
Feminism As Bait 189
The Carnival And Power 193
The Disguises Of Freedom 196
Bibliography 199

VII- Voice of the Quieted Women 203
Indian Wisdom 204

Tear And Smile 211
The Lyre Lurking In Wait For The Arab Woman 214
The Sustained Struggle Of Prose 217
The Tribal Song Of The Body 224
Under The Burka 229
The Son And The Horrible Little One 233
To Die Under The Knife Blows 235
Enemy Bullets 237
The Triumph Of Love 238
Bibliography 241

To Keep the House and Shut One's Mouth

Because just as nature ... made women so that, while shut in, they could keep house, so were they obliged to shut their mouths.

Fray Luis De León

I- The Prism

Fate, that acts as an accomplice, has offered me the following paragraph:

"That the Feminine is the Other! But, my heavens, what is the historical evidence that demonstrates that? What is the text [...] that allows that to be seen? Is it evident in Greek tragedy or in the Bible? Is there a special supplement of the *Decalogue* just for the *Other*?" (11). It's a phrase from Rosa Chacel, from her essay "Late Commentary on Simone de Beauvoir", that, from the beginning, points to several ideas that invite reflection:
The *OTHER*, well, for Rosa Chacel is not the feminine, and nevertheless, she herself, who wrote perhaps the most lucid and unusual pages that have been written about the burning theme of woman's reality in our times, repeated over and over again that woman is different from man, that her body is different as much in its possibilities for the sexual act as in that which has to do with offspring, from which her position in society is derived. In spite of that, she pointed out –and demonstrated, in her book *Saturnal*– that we are in a historical moment in which major changes are being produced that, in part, are focused on precisely the coming together of the sexes, not because of the masculinization of woman but because of the feminization of man.

The difference between man and woman has always existed; it is evident from their bodies. Nevertheless, going back to pre-history, there once was a time in which –apart from the procreating factor– man and woman would accomplish the same tasks. This took place in the arboreal nests period, when man was still the gatherer and would spend the entire day looking for food and, when night fell, would climb up into the trees to sleep. Man and woman, pure nomads, would walk with their children on their back–as long as these were not able to walk– and would gather berries from the bushes, and then, when dark fell, just like some animals, they would climb up to the treetops and rest among the branches. Their life, hard and monotonous, was short, not extending beyond 18 or 20 years.

Things changed as soon as some respite was discovered when hunting was invented: Women did not have –in general– the necessary strength to confront the big animals, and, in addition, they would often be pregnant. From this moment on, everyday tasks of one or the other sex began to be defined. At the beginning there was nothing established, this happened much later. And when that initial necessity was forgotten, the distribution of tasks seemed like something imposed from outside and determinative.

Returning to Rosa Chacel, to the afore-mentioned essay, it is interesting to underscore her response to a phrase by Simone de Beauvoir, cornerstone of the question. The French writer says the following: "The worst curse that weighs on woman is that of having been excluded from war expeditions. Not giving his life but risking it is how man has been elevated to superior to animals; for that reason, superiority has been granted, not to the sex that procreates, but to the one that kills" (12). And Chacel replies: "It is evident that from there stems the supremacy, the real supremacy of the male, and then certainly the female would be something else, she would be "*the Other*", she would not ever be able to feel close to her fellow man if she were not able, in all respects, to carry out that specifically human act of risking one's life voluntarily. But it is not this way: Woman, without exception, can do it; every woman from every class or race is equipped to do so" (12).

The implacable lucidity of the Valladolid writer does not stop there; she continues to open up the way through that intricate pathway: "Of course, what counts for the matter is the real fact of warrior expeditions, but is it that woman was excluded from them? Simone de Beauvoir does not conceive that, for such a number of women, so extensive that one could almost say *the woman*, and women so well constituted mentally, awake, free, the mission of procreating might make sense" (12-13). Effectively, the female was not totally excluded from warrior expeditions; there were, including in the Middle Ages, feminine orders of chivalry.

Rosa Chacel does not give in: "Man assumes the risk for his life and woman assumes the *responsibility* for introducing any number of lives into the world". This is a point that, in reality, is of great importance, because given historical changes –the way of making war– precisely because with each succeeding year the responsibility falls on both sexes, since the risks have been modified. On the other hand, the autonomy of women when confronted with maternity, their possibility of decision-making, makes this such that it does not suppose slavery for one's entire life: having ten or fifteen children is not comparable to having one. In antiquity, only the women who were not completely tied to their tasks, that is, those from the upper class or nuns, were able to become cultured, and these could demonstrate their autonomy and creative forces.

When Ana Comneno (17th Century) decides to undertake her father's biography, that of the Byzantine Emperor Alejo I Comneno, she starts by declaring that she is a cultured woman and has not left rhetoric aside. Such a declaration should not be necessary because, for that person who reads her work, *The Alexíada*, it becomes evident that the author knows her Classical writers, and what writing is, and also that she is a great writer. I say *writer* (as opposed to *woman writer*) because in that immense book of hers she confronts us with a historical process, through court intrigues and, above all, battle stories, and nothing that is particularly feminine comes across in her pages.

The (woman) poet Sappho, many centuries before, did not need to justify her poems in any way, nor the fact of singing or reciting with complete freedom. Her tone and her perspective were, simply, those of her contemporaries. And going back still further, we could almost say that woman is not *the Other* but rather *the One*. To begin, 2,500 years before Christ we find the first known poetic voice, which is precisely feminine: the Akkadian priestess Enheduanna, firm in enunciating and denouncing. Sometime later, in the 10th Century, and taking, as in time, a leap in space, the first great novel of universal literature, according to the way in which we understand the genre today, is the work of the Japanese woman writer Muraski Shikibu: *The History of Genji*, that has been compared with Cervantes' *Don Quixote of la Mancha*, and with Proust's *In Search of Lost Time*. It offers us a backdrop of the society of their time that does not cause us to think about the needle and thread.

During the period of arboreal nests, neither man nor woman knew which was his or her reality, because they were not able to see themselves, and in following periods, when each step taken by those who belonged to one or the other sex was a necessary one, such a theme –to see oneself as male or female– was not considered. Only when the reason that had induced one to establish different conducts according to sex seemed so remote, when that fact became alienating, was it revealed through a new perspective. This perspective achieved high levels of sophistication during the Baroque period, a period in which misogyny was merged with the covering up of the senses, in such a way that it affected forms. Thus did disguise open up a pathway, and at the same time, an incipient feminism.

Today, the panoramas had opened up as if by means of a great cornerstone, and it is logical that women writers would focus their gaze, among other things, toward this aspect of the landscape that surrounds them. The consequence of this vision turns out to be particularly interesting in societies that continue to be subjected to ancestral situations or that have just achieved a certain degree of freedom. We find important examples among contemporary Arab women writers, many of whom include overwhelming books of testimony in their production.

This outlining of the facts and this consciousness are related to phases of development that different peoples have reached. There are still some who find themselves in a previous state, subjected to less "elaborated" cultures. Nevertheless, once the moment has arrived, women throw themselves into the struggle running as much risk as in other acts of life. Curiously, it can happen, as it does in some cases, that they may be creators while man does not do anything other than prepare himself for war. I am referring to Afghan women of the Pashtun language, those who, while being illiterate, are depositories of an extraordinary traditional lyric. In a similar mix of historical strata as seen in present-day situations, to look at the past and its successions can result sometimes, at the very least, as a guiding principle.

Lacan affirmed that the entire problem of the human being resides in the fact that we cannot find a response to the question "what is it to be a man and what is it to be a woman", since neither men nor women are moved as much by sex as animals (15). This is exactly what happens: the element of reason grants us great possibilities of proximity. The Syrian-Lebanese poet Adonis wrote: "Reason is something that we all share, and it's that which we all know. This is what reason offers which is why it does not function as a cognitive method. To know is to know the unknown, and that which is different. We are equal in the realm of reason but different as regards the body. This experience can be seen represented in dreams, in desire, in ecstasy, in movement, in dynamics" (15). Adonis was not referring to the sexes, but instead his lucid reflection introduces us into the following reality: Differences as much as similarities constitute a true richness that we should not easily renounce.

Bibliography

Chacel, R., *Saturnal (Saturnal),* Seix Barral, Barcelona, 1972.

__________. "Artículos I y II" ("Articles I and II"), *0bra completa* (*Complete Work*), Jorge Guillén Foundation, Valladolid, 1993.

II- Priestesses, Courtesans, Princesses and Women in Love: Paradoxical Writing

If we were to ask ourselves about what today we call literature, we would have to remember that before letters were invented, there existed a form of oral expression. And if we looked for that first burst of expression and how it came about, we would probably say that it was born linked to life itself, perhaps to the very act of giving and receiving it, and therefore, that it was born from feminine lips. It would be, without a doubt, a song, a peaceable song, perhaps a lullaby. Afterwards, all members of the community would intone similar songs to placate the forces of nature, unknown elements, or the gods. From these beginnings of oral literature until the actual word could be fixed in stone or on a leaf, thousands of years would pass.

Writing dates from the beginning of the third Millennium before Christ, and I affirm here that the first name of any author we have knowledge of dates from 350 years before. And besides –we are dealing with a female here– the highly respected Akkadian priestess Enheduanna, similar perhaps to that prehistoric Sumerian *bas-relief* that launched into the air a magic ribbon to subdue a bison. That first female poet, from the enclosure of her temple, emitted a strong and solemn voice to impose herself on her suspicious, and sometimes hostile, surroundings.

Taking inspiration from this initial song, let us also launch a magic ribbon into the air in order to bring together these poetic beginnings from the Middle East with those of a more sophisticated feminine writing, that of the Far East, of women from China, Korea and Japan, and we shall see that strange paradoxes result from such a perspective.

Sexualized Writing

As a preparatory step, let us consider the situation from ancient times and the role that the female occupied within it. In those days, the voice of the priestess, a sacred voice, with the character of divine authority, was imperious, while the voice of the common woman was inaudible. Despite everything, no matter how elevated and solemn the voice of the priestess was, if she did communicate, she did not do so at a personal level but rather would follow certain paradigms. Perhaps this is the point from which follows the basic paradox: the voice that "best" expresses itself is not always the one that communicates more.

But let us observe the background that this carries with it; if we leave religious cults to one side, we shall see that in some countries, like Greece or China, throughout some historical periods, the female received education and even her creative ability was considered of great value, while in others she had to be kept enclosed and suppressed and only the female courtesan –aside from the female priest– could have access to culture, almost as if she were a man. This paradox achieves its highest point in the Far East where the division of the sexes applied even to writing. As much as in Korea as in Japan, both a feminine writing and a male one exist.

In these countries, the greatest refinement –and that required of men– was to write in Chinese and in the Chinese way, that is, following a foreign tradition and with some ideograms, that, in fact, were inadequate for their own languages. For this reason, in Korea and Japan respectively, there arose an alphabetic type of writing and another syllabic one, both adapted to the indigenous language and reserved for the "uncultured" women and called "women's writing". Also in China, in the South, there was a "woman's writing" (in reality a language): *Nushu,* utilized in secret. Its signs were phonetic and transmitted from mother to daughter. In *Nushu*, there were prepared what were called "Letters from the Third Day", songs handed over the third day of the wedding celebrations and then burned at the recipient's time of death, to accompany her to the other world. This practice was not ended until the Mao revolution.

Clamor In The Temple

But let us return to the first writer from history with a recognized name, that of Enheduanna. Nothing was known about her until 1926 when Sir Leonard Woolsey discovered an alabaster disk broken into pieces but that carried inscriptions that spoke of the high priestess from Nanna, goddess of the moon, and they were able to reconstruct some of the data. Some fragments from 42 well-known hymns (such as Hymns from the Sumerian Temple) have remained, and these appear under her name and, in fact, did not begin to be studied until the 1960s of the 20th Century.

And let us see how for this first woman writer, the situation becomes controversial. Daughter of King Sargon (2371-2316 B.C.), who founded the Akkadian Empire after conquering the King of Sumer, Enheduanna was named high priestess by her father and she, from her position, supported him in his political objectives. She was poorly received by the male priests, the same ones who apparently destroyed the disk and other writings where she was mentioned in order to destroy her tracks. In fact, it cannot be confirmed 100 per cent that Enheduanna was the textual author of the hymns, for there are those who believe she only compiled them, but what is certain is that in more than one of them she cites herself. Her style follows those of anonymous religious songs –with a tone that is highly evocative because of its repetitions and advocations–, except that in her case it is more sophisticated because, besides a religious dimension, it also contains a political dimension. The priestess, on the other hand, is identified with the goddess (not just of the moon, Nanna, but also of fertility, Inanna) and including, as has been pointed out from the *Hymn to Inanna and Ebih*, she speaks for herself, expressing her confrontation with the priests. She says this in a strophe:

> Since he [Ebih] did not kiss the ground before me,
> nor did he sweep the dust before me with his beard,
> I will raise my hand over this instigating country:
> I will teach it to fear me. (20)

A splendid beginning for the song out of the mouth of a woman, written more than 4,000 years ago with stubborn arrogance. Apparently, the hymn also commemorated Sargon's triumphs and, therefore, the goddess Inanna arises as a fighter and destroyer:

> I will bring war [to Ebih], I will instigate combat,
> I will draw arrows from my quiver,
> I will unleash rocks from my sling as a greeting,
> I will impale [Ebih] with my sword. (20)

The hymn continues with supplications and praises and the moment arrives in which the priestess names herself (as much later, like a rubric, other poets who sing their poems will also do, such as the Sufis and the troubadours), and she says: "I am Enheduanna, the priestess of Nanna" (20).

Together with the petitions and praises, the hymn also describes the development of rites. So it is in these lines, where Esdam-ku is mentioned, that is, Inanna's temple in Girsi/Lagash:

> I have heaped the coals, prepared the purification rites,
> The Esdam-ku stands ready for you.
> Will you not pacify your heart for me? (20)

But perhaps the most triumphant moment of the hymn is the moment of exaltation of the goddess, full of solemnity and crowned with victory:

> Queen of all granted powers
> like the light not hidden behind a candle,
> dressed in splendor, oh infallible,
> sky and heaven are your coverings.

… … … … … … … .
Queen of the essential forces,
warden of the origins of the cosmos,
you who exalt the elements,
tie them to your hands,
guard them in your chest,
oh you who sculpt fire like a dragon,
you fill the earth with your poison
you howl like the god of the storm,
like a seed you lie on the ground.
You are the abundant river that rushes down the mountainside,
you are Inanna,
she who dominates heaven and earth. (20-21)

With A Fish In The Chest

The Sumerian Akkadian hymns have an extraordinary poetic force and in them many themes appear that other literatures will later take and develop, like the deluge or the descent into Hell. And not only are these great themes transmitted but also small details, without a doubt related to shared customs. We see here that the very same Enheduanna, in one line, alludes to the fact that she wears the trappings that correspond to her rank but, for example, in a Hittite hymn the God Telpinu, filled with irritation and in any given moment, puts his right shoe on his left foot and the goddess Anzilli puts her pectoral on backwards and her hair arrangement opposite from how it should be. These last details do not turn out to be so surprising if we think that in Egypt, during the second Millennium before Christ, there appears a curious poem that says:

I have only braided half of my hair
I came in a hurry
and did not take care of my attire. (21)

We understand that a young woman in love, or a lover, apologizes for her distractedness due to impatience. This brief poem, less than a century after Enheduanna's, has nothing to do with those of the Akkadian priestess. The song has now departed from the temple, from the sacred environs, and the verses are a spontaneous expression of intimacy.

Let us take a look now at the Egyptian society. In it, woman occupied an important place: royalty was transmitted by maternal blood and society was fundamentally monogamous, even if the pharaoh was able to have numerous wives, including his sisters and daughters. In fact, the female moved in an equal relationship with the male. Although the pharaohs' village focused all of their acts on the questions of death and the afterlife, it did not appear to be focused on religion. Thus, for example, marriage ceremonies were not carried out. A marriage contract was made up that specified the property for each spouse, and in addition, the possibility of divorce at the request of either spouse also existed, without any guilt having to be established. Nevertheless, marriage was an unquestionable social ideal. The female would act in a manner completely independent from the male, but within family confines. At home she was the "señora" and the husband was subject to her dictates.

In that which is probably the oldest Egyptian book, *The Teachings of Plahhotep*, the husband is warned that he should caress his wife and not treat her with harshness or his life would be ruined. He should open his arms to her, give her proofs of love and buy her perfumes and cosmetics. We have no doubt that this corresponded to the reality, when we find poems like this one:

> My God, how sweet it is for me [——]
> to go to the pond and bathe in front of you,
> showing you my beauty
> wrapped in a fine tunic
> impregnated with fine balsamic essences:
> I will go down to the water and come up again,
> with a red fish,
> very beautiful, between my fingers.
> I will place it on my chest.
> Come and gaze at me! (22)

Together with this suggestive poem, we find, for example, the passionate cry of a young woman who defends her love when faced with her father's censure:

> I will not abandon him,
> even though they strike me [...]
>
> And should I have to spend the whole day in the marsh,
> and even if they pursue me with stakes to Syria,
> or even to Nubia with palm sticks,
> or to the desert with canes,
> or to the shore of the sea hitting me with reeds.
>
> I will not listen to their tricks
> and I will not renounce the man I love. (23)

I Will Climb Up the Erect Palm Tree

More innocent but equally direct were the amorous songs from mouths of women that occurred both in China and India several centuries before Christ, but I do not want to take this leap without mentioning a well-known biblical book, the *Song of Songs* of Solomon, whose origin still sets off polemics. In general, it is thought that the book's sources go back to the times in which sacred prostitution existed, and also that it is derived directly from Egyptian songs and Sumerian-Akkadian hymns to Ishtar, another goddess of fertility. It has, in addition, notable similarities, because of its themes and its stylistic form, with the poems collected together in the *Tolkappiyam*, a compendium of grammar and literature that is the oldest written in the *tamil* language.

Whatever may be its origin, and although later it might have been interpreted from a divine point of view, owing to the fact that already in the First Century before Christ it seemed scandalous to the Jews, the *Song of Songs* is, clearly, an epithalamium. And it turns out to be almost impossible to see its highly erotic metaphors any other way, beginning with those that appear in the suggestive beginning, set in the mouth of the wife (I use here Fray Luis de León's translation): "May my lover kiss me with his mouth, / his loves are sweeter than wine", including the ones that follow, as in the praise of the spouse by her companions:

> Your navel is a circular cup,
> full of a very valued sweet liquor;
> a mountain of wheat is your beautiful belly,
> surrounded by violets, and scented.

Your breasts, in beauty and tenderness,
two joyful twin baby goats;
[…]
Oh, how pretty you are and bestowed,
a friend and very valued in delights,
a very beautiful palm tree, and very grown,
your presence seems so esteemed,
very girded by some sweet bunches
which are your breasts, oh bride.
I said: "I will climb up the erect palm tree,
And I will grab the beloved's bunches". (24)

The tone of exaltation is spread throughout the *Song of Songs*, but in it we also detect quotidian and more generalized customs appropriate of the female, such as going out covered up –for the woman in love wounds the heart of her spouse "with only one eye"–, and its preferable reclusiveness. Thus, when the spouse says "small is our sister", he responds:

We will build a very strong wall,
and I would make him a silver palace;
and we will build on cedar doors;
and she enclosed within the palace,
will be very safe and very well guarded. (24)

The oldest Jewish cabalists, as contrary to the Rabbinical hierarchies, did not fear eroticism, Gershom Sholem says to us: "They never interpreted the *Song of Songs* as a dialogue between God and the soul, that is to say, like an allegorical description of the road to arrive at the *mystical union*, the common interpretation for Christian mystics since the time of St. Bernard of Claravaux. The Mystic School of Safed from the 16th Century was the first to feel itself attracted by this interpretation" (25).

The alchemists, for their part, incorporated the protagonists and metaphors from the mystical union, such as the famous couple of the king and queen that together make up the philosopher's stone. In *Aurora consurgens*, that enigmatic book attributed to St. Thomas of Aquinas, the steps to reach that stone are outlined, and images and equivalent concepts are utilized, transferred to the different phases of the work, such as *nigredo*, *rubedo* o *albedo,* since "that which elevates the soul will see the colors". The entire suggestive text leads to that definitive union, "strong like death (25)".

If we think, therefore, that the origin of the *Song of Songs* stems from Egyptian songs or Sumerian Akkadian hymns, its eroticism strikes us as natural. And one ought not to omit that it is a song in dialogue between the voices of the male spouse, the female spouse and the companions, which gives it richness, above all upon hearing it sung, as without a doubt the hymns of Enheduanna were sung. If Solomon were the one who had really composed it, it would date from the year 1020 B.C. but, because of its twists and Armenian references, it appears that its writing dates from the 4th Century B.C.. In this case, it would be a contemporary of the Hindu poems from the *Tolkappiyam*, those to which I have referred, situated between the 4th and 3rd Centuries B.C., and also, probably collected together in the *Kuruntokai*, like those written before in Tamil and proceeding from an oral tradition, but collected then between the 3rd Century B.C. and the 3rd Century A. D.. It would be, on the other hand, clearly posterior to many of the Chinese poems from the *Shi Jing* (*Book of Model Poems*), that dates between the 9th and 6th Centuries B.C..

The Ingenuous Song

Our attention is called to the fact that, throughout different periods in history, there appear songs emanating from the mouths of women –for example in Medieval Spain, the *jarchas,* or the poems already mentioned from India (above all those making up the *Kuruntokai*)– and that the name of the author is not known. It seems evident that a woman was the one singing them. It is another question if later a scribe would write them down or a poet would incorporate them into his poems. Without a doubt because of their spontaneity, the anonymous poems from the *Shi Jing* seem to be closer to us and, on the other hand, they can be situated, as I was saying, between the 9th and 6th Centuries B.C. One of them says the follows:

I beg you, Zhonzi,
that you not scale the wall of the town.
Do not break our willows.
It is not that they are not important to me,
but I am afraid of my parents.
Even though I love you with all my soul,
I am afraid of what they are going to say.

I beg you, Zhonzi,
that you not jump over the fences of my house,
nor that you break my mulberries.
It is not they are not important to me,
but I am afraid of my sisters.
Even though I love you with all my soul,
I am afraid of what they are going to say.

I beg you, Zhonzi,
that you not jump over the garden walls,

nor break our elm trees.
It is not that they are not important to me,
but I am afraid of what people might say.
Even though I love you with all of my soul,
I am afraid of malicious tongues. (26)

It is apparent –to the ear– that we are dealing with some verses of great freshness, comparable to those of the *jarchas* or those collected together in the *Kuruntokai*, as we can see in a poem belonging to this collection, selected by chance:

What she said:
(to her friend so that he could hear her)
What evil is there in this,
friend?
If you tell him:
"Oh, man of the hills,
now you come at midnight,
a dark and dangerous midnight,
when in the forest, the black tiger,
that excellent hunter,
suffers the ire of the strong elephant with the long trunk
and longs to ambush the red dog
with humid eyes.
Don't come then!
Her mother said to her
that she throw out the small parrots with the curved beaks
from the ripe wheat". (27)

These poems that are so ancient and so direct and simple do not cease to amaze us, sung by girls who were more or less ruffians, even though nothing is said of their authorship.

On the other hand, very different are the poems from women authors known by their first and last names from the 6th Century B.C. in Greece such as Sappho, and these texts of women writers from Alexandria, a city where, after the death of Alexander the Great, in 323 B.C., the female had greater autonomy. In this city there had begun an emancipation movement whose most representative figure –and here we take a great leap in time– would be the philosopher Hypatia, already from the 5th Century of our era. This movement was aborted by Christianity, that, converted in official religion, pursued the pagans, causing a great many martyrs, among them the very same Hypatia who, harassed by a gang of fanatics, was brutally assassinated.

Norms For Women's Rooms

Let us turn our attention to the Far East, where in the same period, that is during the 5th Century A.D., the flower of paradox was opening. China was experiencing, at that time, the period that was called the "Six Dinasties (229-588 A.D.). The society had evolved notably since the times of the song of the ingenuous *Shi Jing*, and along with the common woman, wife and mother of the family, there arose a class of cultured courtesan women (as also happened in Korea and Japan), highly thought of because of their talent. I have mentioned this point already: The courtesans were valued because of their culture, while the more common women were not allowed to express themselves: it often happened that they would have to burn their poems –or that their parents would do it– so that the family not become disrespected. This, apparently, with some notable exceptions, lasted until the Ching Dynasty (Manchu, 1644-1911), that broke with taboos and when the capacity of the upper class female to write poetry was even considered a part of the dowry. During that time, and based on their merits, a woman poet could be named by the emperor as a "Court Intellectual". But this dynasty was an exception. In fact, the Chinese woman, throughout 2,000 years, did not occupy official positions and she could only be a wife, concubine, maid, Buddhist nun, Taoist priest, courtesan, prostitute, housekeeper, matchmaker or midwife. In general, only the nuns, female priests, and courtesans were cultured; the rest were given just enough education to allow them to read manuals of behavior for women.

According to *The Book of Rituals*, attributed to Confucius, when she was seven, the girl was separated from boys (with the exception of close relatives) and confined in rooms for women. This did not take place with families of farmers, artisans or merchants, where girls helped with the jobs and enjoyed a greater freedom. For the daughters of imperial bureaucrats, on the contrary, things were very different. For example: they could only travel in a hand chair or a carriage with curtains and only to visit temples or relatives. In any case, marriages were arranged and the bride and groom, in general, would not see each other until the day of the wedding. If the wife were not pleasing to him, the groom could take in concubines. She, on the other hand, was submitted to the caprice of her husband and the control of the mother-in-law, whom she was obligated to serve and to groom.

In the aforementioned manuals, *Norms for Women's Rooms* (16th Century) and, concretely, in *Precepts for Women*, one reads that the virtues of these women "are not the brilliant talent nor the distinction or elegance, but rather the reserve, calm, chastity, quiet, and self-control in order to contain the sense of shame and a behavior according to the Confucian norms of etiquette" (29).

This rigidity did not dominate in all of China and its immediate surroundings. The Naxi, inhabitants of the region of Lijiang, that extends from the foot of the great mountain range to the Northwest of Yunnan, before losing their autonomy, they enjoyed some customs so open that they allowed for free love. Among them, the woman, the center of society, could choose her own mate from the time she was 16, and having illegitimate children was not the reason for shame or repudiation. This particular group of people, upon losing their independence and being submitted to laws of the Han, among which were included the obligation of engagement and monogamous matrimony, without any possibility of an ulterior relationship, responded with a dizzying increase of ritualistic suicides among one or several pairs of lovers.

The Naxi's religious beliefs identified suicide as a form of transformation of the spirits in demons capable of causing grave harm to the families or to the community, and for that reason it was necessary to carry out a ceremony that was merciful for the suicidal spirits. The people's oral tradition would collect these events in histories, that later became part of some manuscripts from the *dongba* culture[1], integrated with the Naxi. These aforementioned manuscripts were achieved with pictograms, and their text is not simply narrative, but rather has a liturgical and ritualistic function. Among them is included the beautiful *Kamegiumiky*, that narrates the suicide of a girl.

Subtlety and Impulse

In spite of some very strict precepts regarding women, in the Chinese anthologies there remain some poems spun from the feminine pen, sometimes connected to surprising stories. The first woman poet considered of any importance in said literature, Ts'ai Yen, was the daughter of a writer. It was around the year 195 A.D. –that is, end of the 2nd Century– that she was captured by the Huns, taken to the North and turned into a concubine for the little boss to whom she gave two children. Sometime later she was rescued by the founder of the Wei Dynasty, Ts'ao Ts'ao, a friend of her father. The children stayed back. She relates it in a lively poem:

> A Tartar boss forced me to be his wife,
> and he took me far away, to the edge of the sky.
> 10,000 clouds and mountains
> cut off the road to my land and swirls of dust
> and sand blow in 1,000 leagues. Here the men
> are as savage as giant snakes
> and they show off clad in armor and making their
> bows crackle.

1 The name *dongba* goes back especially to the religious-Shamanic traditions, to the priests who officiated the rites or to their writing.

While I sing the second verse,
I almost break the lute strings.
Without will, I with my heart broken, I sing for myself. (30)

During the T'ang Dynasty (618-905), a period for poetry of great flourishing, as I have pointed out, the courtesan women who would perform at parties and official banquets and belonged to expensive brothels, frequented by functionaries and even the emperor, achieved great standing. Those endowed with great talent were treated like equals and participated in the poetic contests. Many were respected as concubines by the powerful men. But, as regards woman in general, the laws were enormously discriminatory, and said for example: "f a husband attacks and wounds his wife, his punishment will be two degrees below that which corresponds to such a crime. If a husband attacks and gravely wounds his concubine, his penalty will be two degrees lower than the one corresponding for the husband who injures his wife" (30), "If a woman attacks her husband, she will be punished with slave work for a year (a punishment seven degrees above that of a man). If the husband is gravely injured, the sentence will be three degrees higher (which means slave work for two years, a punishment nine degrees above that given a man, 30-31)". Given that panorama, the Taoist women priests, among which were princesses and wealthy women, were the ones who enjoyed the greatest freedom not to become anyone's property. In addition, contrary to Buddhist women nuns, they could have intimate relationships with men and were very sought after as sexual initiators.

In fact, throughout the history of China, great changes regarding the possibilities of women were produced, related to events and reigning philosophies –Confucianism or Taoism–. The greatest Chinese woman poet of all times, Li Qingzhao (1083-1151) was born in the Song Dynasty, during the years when diverse movements of peoples modified the borders to the North and the Emperor expanded in the South (1127-1279). Li Qingzhao, married to a writer and bibliophile, had a happy marriage. Both were dedicated to study and to cataloguing inscriptions, and they grew to have a library that occupied 10 rooms. With the invasions, they were obligated to leave their house, but they took with them 15 carriages of books, calligraphies and art objects. Shortly after, he died, and she, having lost everything, wandered through different cities in search of shelter. Nothing is known about her last years. Some poems remained, of an extraordinary elegance. They were written in large part following the *ci* system, which means that they were written for a known melody, and they have been beautifully translated to Spanish by Pilar González España.

What does Li Qingzhao transmit to us fundamentally? Her interior voice, profound, is born moved by the call of her surroundings. It has to do with an atmosphere that vibrates in each work and that becomes an accomplice: space rises up through the capturing of the senses (colors, perfumes, tastes, touch) and also time; the time of day and night; the time measured by clepsydras, the season, eclosion or the withering of flowers, the blooming of flowers, and the falling of leaves. In her verse, Li Qingzhao begins by defining some basic points of knowledge, for example, the four elements: water in the shape of rain, dew, tears, lakes; air in the wind, hurricanes, the flights of birds, fire in the flames, smoke, embers in incense; earth where the leaves grow, grasses, where there are mountains, unlimited horizons, grass for the sleep of herons and seagulls, and that in winter becomes a "green carpet". And she, the poet, is in the middle, turned into a loving offering. She wrote this poem for the melody that lends its title:

> Collecting blackberries
> In the twilight
> gusts of wind and rain
>
> burning light that comes apart
> and burns out
>
> I have already stopped playing the bamboo flute
>
> and in front of the mirror set in flowers
> I apply my makeup lightly
>
> under the dress of purple silk
> my fine skin of snow
> exhales a delicious perfume
>
> then, smiling
> I whisper to my beloved sweetly:
>
> "Tonight
> behind the muslin canopy
> we will feel the freshness of our bed". (32)

Perhaps this is the reality that penetrates so deeply into us, the fact that she herself, the poet, is joined with the atmosphere, and, at the same time, the surroundings reflect her state of being, since, next to the lotus, aloe incense or trees, there are flutes of barbarians approaching, closed doors or open, dawn and dusk, drunkenness from wine and lights, shadows moved by the wind and their uncombed tresses, their golden hairpins, their suits of silk, the jade cauldrons, the cups, the bed with blankets and sheets. And the clairvoyance that goes well beyond.

Now let us take another leap in time to arrive at the year 1800, around the time another lyrical voice saw the light: Wu Tasao, poet who, because of her impetus, particularly attracts one's attention. Daughter and wife of a business man; abused by one and the other, she lost interest in men and had lots of friends and women lovers for whom she wrote poems, often erotic, that were very popular and were sung throughout China. Unexpectedly, around 1837 she became a Taoist priest and retreated to a reclusive site. Her way of expressing herself is colloquial above all and very different from that utilized by the majority of Chinese women poets. Thus, also in the *ci* style, that is, to be sung, concretely the melody "The Love of Immortals," she wrote the poem:

> To the Courtesan Ch'ing Lin
> Above your svelte body the necklaces
> adornments of jade and coral from your belt
> ring like those of a a woman friend
> may she come from the City of Jade.
> When we see each other, your smile
> leaves me mute and I forget the words. You have spent
> too much time gathering flowers and
> reclined against the bamboo and your sleeves
> have become cold, in your valley
> deserted: I see you totally alone, a girl
> who harbors cryptic thoughts.

You shine like a perfumed lamp in the
shadows that are becoming too dense. We play
at drinking and reciting our poems to each other.
Then you sing: "Memories from the south of the river",
with your piercing verses. Then we paint our
precious eyebrows. I want to possess you
completely: your jade body and
your promised heart. It is spring.
Great clouds cover the Five Lakes.
Beloved, let me buy
a boat painted red and carry you away from here. (33-34)

Korean Courtesan Women

The educational paradox that was lived in China between the common woman and the courtesan also took place in Korea, where, on the one hand, there existed an entire literature directed against the mother-in-law, who was the one, in fact, who governed harshly during the engagement period. The situation of the courtesans was very different. These, called *kisaeng,* inscribed in a society that followed Confucian doctrines, were cultured entertainers of literati cults and, although in this country there were no pleasure neighborhoods, like in China or Japan, these women worked through the civil servants and were even regulated by the public administration. They were recruited as children, at an age of between 10-15, through complicated selection that was carried out by law every three years at the national level, and they were taught singing, dancing, writing and the art of entertaining.

The rigid Confucian norms –filial piety and feminine chastity– limited woman's sphere of action to inside the house, with explicit prohibition for widows of contracting second nuptials. In a document of *Sin Sukchu* from the 15th Century, one reads: "In general, people know how to educate their children, but not their daughters. A woman is loyal and pure, she controls her emotions, she adapts and is obedient and serves others. She takes care exclusively of domestic affairs and does not get involved in public ones" (34). From there the contrast of the common woman (who, if she learned to read or write, it was in hiding) with the *kisaeng*, who could even write in Chinese following the models of Li Bai, Du Fu or Su Dongpo, and that, according to their beauty and aptitude, were inscribed on the lists where government officials were also included. In this case, a Far East paradox is clear-cut.

The Korean language, like the Japanese, as we have seen, did not adapt to Chinese ideograms. For this reason there's a great difference between the poems in which the *sijo* is used –the women's alphabet– characters that are fresher and more spontaneous than those embodied in *hansi* –Chinese writing, also called *real* or *true*–. The poems of the *kisaeng*, on the other hand, were sung. [2] The writings in *sijo* lacked a title, and we see one from Hongjang (15th Century):

> In the Pavilion of the Pine of Winter
> on a night of full moon,
> when the waves die down,
> against the hill of the Splendorous Waterfall,
> the faithful white gulls come and go,
> how can my beloved have left and not returned? (35)

2 There exists a splendid anthology done by the Italian Vicenza d'Urso, *Canto dal padiglione azzuro* (where the oldest poet is from the 14th Century), that I take as a point of reference.

A century later Hwang Chini would write:

> Terse and transparent water, that runs among the green mountains,
> do not be too vain to descend them quickly.
> When you are united with the great blue sea,
> you will not be allowed to return.
> The white moon shines full, like empty mountains.
> What would you say about resting a little
> before continuing your rapid journey. (35)

From the woman poet Songi, about whom we know nothing, come these unusual verses:

> How will love be, round or square?
> Long or short? Will it be measurable?
> I do not know its dimension,
> but I still do not see the end. (35)

And from the very same Songi, the following:

> Rooster, do not sing,
> do not be so vain as to sing soon,
> you are not the Prince Maeng Chang di Qi.
> My beloved is coming today:
> what would you say about not singing at all? (36)

Now, so that the contrast between these poems with those written in China can be seen, I offer one below in *hansi*, of Ch'uhyang, which only tells us that she was of Changsong. The poems in ideograms carry a title:

> In the Changam Pavilion
> Noise of oars in the tranquil estuary:
> surprised, the little nocturnal heron awakens and takes off flying.
>
> The mountains are ignited with the autumnal red color.

The sand is clear: from the moon it has no shadow.
(36)

Rarely does eroticism flourish in these poems, but on occasion there can be detected a certain margin of movement that is highly insinuating. Thus, the poet Yi Kyesaeng, also known as Maech'ang, expressed herself in *hansi*, at the end of the 16th Century:

Dedicated to a Drunken Guest

The drunken guest grabs onto the dress of silk,
the silk dress is adjusted to the hand that tears it.
The dress is not important to me,
what I fear is the end of love. (36)

To Say And To Tell

The force of a poem such as that of Yi Kyesaeng is based on its brevity that increases the effectiveness of the word. In Japan, the word is endowed with another power. In the year 300 B.C., the harvest of rice arrives at the Japanese archipelago and with it begin liturgies associated with agriculture, in which shorter, disconnected sentences are used, sometimes disconnected from their meaning and endowed with such force that they allow for the verb to have attributed to it a magical capacity. It is like this to such an extent that one could come to believe that it has a spirit – the *kotodama*. This spirit or power of words (comparable only to that which grants the Hebraic Kabbalah to letters) is of great importance with the appearance, much later (the oldest date of its existence is the year 683 A.D.), of a figure of great importance in relation to woman and literature in the country: the *kataribe*. The scholar Kayoko Takagi defines it in this way: "An official appointment boasted by that person that could recite histories about the origins of the lineage of the royal family" (37). In any case, in general this position was held by women. And there was more: in the same way that in other civilizations the shaman was the one who could realize the relationship between the divine and this world, in Japan the mediators of divine words, in whose body divinity was incarnated, were the *miko*, female priests, who could be of such high rank as the emperor's sister and whose influence was enormous, for their vehicle was the verb, without doubt, so sacred as Enheduanna's.

These facts were connected to oral transmission, to those words that contained the spirit of the god lodged in the *kotodama*. One of its consequences was that, since the 8th Century, there took hold the custom that women tutors were the ones who educated the children from good families. In reality, Japan, at its beginnings, was close to being a matriarchal society. (It was a female emperor, Jingu—one should not forget—who, in the 3rd and 4th Centuries, conquered Korea).

Due to the fact that since the 6th Century, Chinese characters and the corresponding literary style entered the Japanese archipelago, education soon presented two faces: Chinese writing and oral transmission. But at the end of the 8th Century, there was formed the syllabic writing, *kana*, that, as we have seen, just like the *sijo*, the Korean alphabet, adapted well to the autonomous language, that is, it allowed one to write what was transmitted orally. *Kana* is, then, women's writing in opposition to the *kanji*, the Chinese writing in which man was to express himself. Thanks to this limitation on Chinese imposed on the male, another beautiful paradox –that is, thanks to the use of a different writer for each sex, there arose, already in the 10th century, and from the pen of a woman, Murasaki Shikibu, the first great modern novel, *The Tale of Genji*. The prose of Japanese women is so important that –in the same epoch as Murasaki, for example, Sei Shonagon writes *The Pillow Book*–, that overshadows her lyrical creation. And with everything, poetry was of common use in the court, and therefore a known medium, –and so we see that *The Tale of Genji* is full of poems, in the way of pictures, capturing an instant–.

In the oldest compilation of Japanese writings, the *Manyoshu* (from the beginning of the 8th Century), a third of the voices is feminine. The compendium cannot be more democratic: emperors, warriors, soldiers, beggars, monks and nuns, princesses and courtesans. This particular work dates from a moment in which men and women had freedom of movement to such an extent that the women could even attend hunting expeditions, and of course, appear publicly in the court. Among the interesting women poets is the princess Nukada, who lived in the 7th Century, in a tumultuous period.

Two centuries after the *Manyoshu* –in the 10th Century, already in the Heian period– there is compiled another anthology, the *Kokinshu*, a "collection of antique and modern poems (38)", that incorporates written texts in *kana*. In it there are four times more women than men, but in the works of both there is detected an equal sensibility and culture. In contrast to the *Manyoshu*, the *Kokinshu* is saturated with ideas from the Buddhist aesthetics—*mono no aware*—, a response of refined sensibility to the ephemeral, among other things, that of beauty. The verses, following the Chinese custom, appear grouped around the theme of the seasons of the year, and the dominant poetic style is the *waka*, a poem anterior to the appearance of the *haiku*, that consists of 31 syllables arranged in 5—7—5—7—7 – which will later be called *tanka*–. Two women creators stand out in this anthology, both from the 9th Century: Ono no Komachi and the woman Ise, the former more sensual, the latter more intellectual. Let us see quickly some examples. From Ono no Komachi:

> He is not coming.
> Tonight in the darkness of the moon,
> I awaken desiring him.
> My breasts throb and flash,
> my heart is burning. (39)
>
> From Ise:
> Since "the pillow knows all"
> we sleep without a pillow.
> My reputation
> still reaches the skies
> like a dust storm. (39)

One of the great Japanese love poets (Izumi Shikibu) is from the 11th Century. She figures in another florilegium, *Goshui-Wakashu*, and has been compared to Gaspara Stampa and Louise Labé. Izumi Shikibu, by the way, was married several times and was the only one in the Heian period to be censured for promiscuity. And, despite everything, how subtle this *waka* of hers turns out to be:

> With longing for love
> I listen to the monk's bell.
> I will never forget you,
> not even for a moment
> as short as the ones between the sounds of the bell. (39)

But the Heian period (794-1192) is extinguished, the emperors leave their government in the the hands *of shoguns*, crude military men, and in society there prevails the samurai code. Woman is repressed and the independent woman writer is, in general, at this moment, a nun. After a brief renaissance of the lyric, the contemporary poet Ikuki Atsumi affirms that "one can say that during the 700 years of war and military government Tokugawa, there does not appear even a single woman writer of importance". The situation, as in the case of China, is due to the philosophical tenets: now there rule erroneous interpretations of Buddhism and Confucian teachings of submission and annihilation of the feminine "I".

Murasaki

But we have left behind the prose writer Murasaki Shikibu, author of *The Tale of Genji*, that great and gallant novel that dates from the 10th Century and has been compared to Cervantes' *Don Quixote of the Mancha*, Proust's *In Search of Lost Time*, or Boccaccio's *Decameron*. *TheTale of*

Genji is written with such agility and enchantment that it seduces the reader irremediably. Many of the themes that come up in the novel will become independent later, passing to other works, for example to pieces of the Noh theater, one of which, *Aoi no Ue*, deals with Genji, the shining prince, and his lover Rokujo, who, converted into a phantom vampire, turns Aoi, wife of Genji› into a martyr until causing her death. In the novel, this episode begins with a reflection of Rokujo. A few paragraphs are enough to capture all of the subtlety and nuances of Murasaki's writing:

> That night a letter reached him:
>
> "Although it seemed that Aoi had improved, the situation has changed and she is worse than ever. I cannot leave her alone" (40).

The usual excuses, thought Rokujo, but she wrote to him:

> Now it falls to me to undo the road of love.
> with humid sleeves,
> and to walk beyond,
> toward the muddy fields....
> Such a pity that your well has so little water! (40)

Two paragraphs further on, Murasaki introduces, in a progressively more intense way, the phantom vampire:

> In the Sanjo palace, the malign spirit became progressively more active and Aoi worsened right before everyone's eyes. There was no lack of rumors that pointed to Rokujo, insinuating that the torturous spirit was from her or her father, the defunct prince.

> Meanwhile, the accused woman tried to analyze in great detail her feelings toward Aoi [...]. She began to have a recurrent dream: In the magnificently furnished lady's room that Rokujo identified with her rival, she shook her and beat her violently ... it was terrible! At times she would act disconcerted, as if her soul had left her body and was acting on its own. The world did not often speak well of people who had done much worse things. If Aoi died, everyone would point at her. It was not uncommon that the spirits of the dead, offended in life, would continue dragging themselves through the world for revenge. It had always seemed to her somewhat odious, but I maintain here that it was her turn to protagonize a situation like that before dying... (41)

The narrator then goes on to expose the protagonist's sentiments, with a style so artistic that it seems to us we can see the complete portrait:

Profoundly restless, Genji would send messengers to Rokujo's home with great frequency.

Neither in his spouse, that worried him much more, did he note signs of improvement. [...] The long and thick braid that fell on one side of her face stood out against the white of her face and the bed clothing. On that occasion she seemed to him much more beautiful than when she appeared before him completely dressed, but glacial like an ice floe, and he grasped her hand:

> "How terrible!" –sighed the dying one–. —How terrible all of this is for you! [...]
> And with a soft and affectionate voice she recited:
> —Sew the hem of my skirt

> so that the sorrowful soul
> not escape
> for it wants to flee to another place! (41)

> That was not Aoi's voice nor her form of speaking. Genji warned suddenly that the voice belonged to Rokujo and remained petrified. He had heard tell that those things happened, but they always seemed superstitions only accepted by vulgar and ignorant people. And behold that, before his very eyes, he had palpable proof that that monstrous phenomenon that they had described turned out to be perfectly possible. (42)

If the narrator, instead of Muraski, had been a male, would he have captured so well the importance of the phantom –of repressed desires–, that is so well detected through these lines?

The One Hundred Nights

Compared with a writing so fresh and exquisite as is Murasaki's, there also appears in Japan that of the *geishas*. In contrast to the Korean courtesans, the geishas have not disappeared, they continue to be those professional "entertainers", with their impeccable manners, such that the goal is the perfection and harmony of their gestures. Their fundamental task is to carry out the tea ceremony, although they need to be ready to offer sexual services. Their refined culture includes knowing how to sing, dance and write poetry. Due to their moderation and containment, one would not anticipate a poem like this one among their writings:

The love from a little while ago
and the tabacco smoke
little by little
only leaves ashes. (42)

The *geisha* poems –I am basing this fundamentally on those collected by Ikuko Atsumi, previous, of course, to the First World War–, in contrast to those written by the Korean courtesans, do not go beyond the conventional and are all anonymous. One could say that that apprenticeship, that "control" that is necessary for these women, causes them not to go beyond that which is already established, not even in poetry.

Let us turn our attention again, one more time, to the call of love inspiration, to that poet who stands out in the *Kokinshu*, Ono no Komachi:

On my breast
floats a boat of sorrow
and I have just embarked;

Thinking only about him
I fell asleep. And then
he appeared before me.
If I had known that it was a dream
I would never have awakened.

I feel so alone
that my body is floating grass
cut off from its roots.
If there were water that invited me
I believe that I would follow it.

In this night without moonlight
I do not manage to meet him,
I get up sighing
and I feel my chest burn like a flame
my heart devoured by the fire. (43)

Ono no Komachi takes her inspiration from that hope of a love encounter, which elevates the tragedy. According to the legend –that passed into literature– beautiful and distant, she put her beloved, the Captain Fukakusa, to a test, demanding of him that he visit her 100 nights before she would make love to him. He appeared 99 nights but when the 100th night arrived, he did not appear. Ono no Komachi did grow old waiting for him; her body, made to love, would go crazy from longing, and also her poet's soul. When old age arrived, according to the theatrical Noh by Kanami, she said –and we could make a chorus of her words by way of a gentle lament:

The branches that I gather
are to make firewood,
what a pity that they are not
to perfume my sleeves! (44)

Bibliography

Aquinas, St. Thomas of, *Aurora Consurgens. The Rising Dawn*. Marie–Louise Von Franz: edition, translation and commentary of an alchemical treatise attributed to St. Thomas of Aquinas, La Fontaine de Pierre, Paris, 1982.

Barco de orquídeas, Poetisas de China (Orchid Boat: Women Poets of China), ed. K. Rexroth and Ling Chung, Gadir, Madrid, 2007.

Canti del Padiglione Azzuro. Poesie di cortigiane coreane. (Songs of the Padiglione Azzurro. Poetry from the Korean Courtesans). Ed. Vicenza D'Urso, Carmanica Editore, Marina Minturno, 2005.

El suicidio y el canto. Poesía popular de las mujeres pashtún de Afganistan. (Suicide and Song. Popular Poetry of the Pashtun Women of Afghanistan). Ediciones del Oriente y del Mediterráneo, Guadarrama, 2002.

Enheduanna, http: //www. angelfire. com/mi/enheduanna/enhedwriting. html.

González Valles, J., *Filosofía de las artes japonesas (Philosophy of the Japanese Arts)*, Verbum, Madrid, 2009.

Janés, C., *La voz de la mujeres acalladas (Voice of the Silenced Women)*, adamaRamada, Madrid, 2008.

Kuruntokai, ed. of Dr. M. Shumugam Pillai, Koodal Publishers, Madurai, 1976. *La poesia erótico–amorosa en el Egipto Faraónico* (*Erotic Love Poetry in Pharaonic Egypt*), edition and translation by Esteban Llagostera, Esquío, El Ferrol, 1995.

Lanzaco Salafranca, F., *Los valores estéticos de la cultura clásica japonesa (Aesthetic Values of the Japanese Classical Culture)*, Verbum, Madrid, 2009.

Li Qingzhao, *Poesía completa*. (*60 poemas para cantar*), (*Complete Poetry*. *60 Poems to Sing*), Ediciones del Oriente y del Mediterráneo, Guadarrama, 2010.

Mariaselvam, A. *The Song of Songs and Ancient Tamil Love Poems*: *Poetry and Symbolism*. Analecta Bíblica 118, Instituto Bíblico, Rome, 1988.

Murasaki Shikibu, *La historia de Genji* (*Genji's Story*), version of Jordi Fibla, Atalanta, Vilaür,

___________. *La novela de Genji* (*Genji's Novel*), version Xavier Roca–Ferrer, Destino, Barcelona, 2005.

Scholem, G. *Las grandes tendencias de la mística judía (Great Tendencies of Mystic Judaism)*. Siruela, Madrid, 1996.

Ono No Komachi, http: //www. gotterdammerung. org/ japan/literature/ononokomachi.

Woman Poets of Japan, ed. Kenneth Roxroth and Ikiko Atsumi, New Directions Books, New York, 1977.

Takagi, J. "Introducción" a *El cuento del Cortador de Bambú* ("Introduction:" to *the Story of the Bamboo Cutter)*, Cátedra, Madrid, 2004.

III- With The Harmonious From The Sea:

Woman and Writing in Greece and Rome

Perhaps the first description of passion carried out in the West can be found in this poem from Sappho:

> He seems like the gods
> the man I see seated in front of me
> listening absorbed to the sweet sound
> of your voice.
>
> And of your loving laughter that, I swear,
> has shocked the heart in my chest,
> well, if I look at you for a moment, I can
> no longer say anything;
>
> my tongue is breaking, a subtle fire
> travels to the edge of my skin, my eyes
> do not see anything, my ears
> buzz,
>
> a cold sweat covers me, tremors
> seek out all of me, more than the green grass
> I become pallid and believe
> myself to be dead already. (47)

Poetry had not been until then a cry from the heart and, even less, the expression of that which takes place in the body –eyes, ears, tongue, skin, tremors and even that overwhelming feeling that leaves one like death, the loss of breath that can cause love–. Sappho therefore represents a break; a break that, in accord with that definitive phrase from Santayana, for which intelligence is a "graft of passion", turns out to be conducive to lucidity. It is not surprising that this should happen in Greece, the cradle of clarity in thought.

Islands And Fragments

The voice of this woman poet born in Lesbos emerged when (at the end of the 7th Century B.C.), precisely in the same area, there arose what can be considered the first Western poetry. Plato said that "when someone connects the beauty of this world and, remembering the true one, wings are born to him". (48) This initial poetry incorporated the gift of wings and began to expand freely. This was due, perhaps, to what was springing up in the islands, given their geographical condition, their climate and their proximity to the East –Lydia specifically– from which there was arriving a different form of delicacy, elegance and spirituality. The cities of the Aegean and Ionian colonies were younger and less austere than the Peloponnesian ones. One could say that it was precisely the colonizers, who had less rigorous customs, who created, with their vigor –their passion– the authentic life and Greek culture: the art, science, philosophy and poetry. Will

Durant affirms: "The Greek civilization was inherited from its daughters through the mother cities". (48) That was how it developed in the Cyclades islands, in the Sporades, in Crete or Roda, and even in Sicily, in the Magna Grecia.

The islands, then, gently rocked by the sea in their surroundings, were favorable to song and, while the poems preserved in their entirety from these initial times are few, the fragments that are left, like islands surrounded by ellipsis, are sufficient. Returning to Sappho, we read suddenly, for example, that among her verses are these words in the air: " ... and Lydia's beautiful skin adornment covered her feet ..." (49) In spite of how truncated this pronouncement is, it appears to us to be something perfect, as much for its concept as for its manner. The same thing happens with this verse: "and the golden chickpeas would grow along the shores ..." (49) It happens that these fragments appear as evocative spaces in spite of their erased angles, which happens, in general, in all of ancient art. In the Parthenon friezes we see a rider who lifts a perfect arm, while the shoulder is not visible, or the headless Panateneas; or in front of Skopa's Ménade, as it has reached us, we capture its orientation, in spite of the missing parts, pure energy that conquers that lacking from the form. That which today is offered up to our eyes, in these works, is the impeccable gesture of the hand, the fall of some folds, or the body movement that emerges, rises up and turns. And through that fragment, in part, we can know the whole, because that which we perceive is the flame that burns in the matter, the same one that gave life to the work in its totality. Those truncated spaces, equivalent to the ellipsis, invite us to discover their "true" beauty, the one Plato spoke of. And so we recreate it. Sappho again:

> Surround with wreaths, Oh Dica,
> your beautiful hair,
> braiding strands of dill
> with your tender hands,
> because the happy graces
> welcome she who adorns herself with flowers;
> they reject she who does not wear wreaths. (49)

Few we need, then, –some poems, or verses–, to enter into that idyllic world toward which the poet Sappho carries us so naturally. Perhaps in that naturalness resides the assessment of love that arises in those songs –a feeling moved by the beauty (and the person), that is beyond gender–, so that one can consider Sappho as a "true prophet of love in the West" (Schadewaldt), and also as a precursor of Plato (49).

Sappho was born in Lesbos, in the year 602 B.C., and as a little girl she went to live in Mytilene. Daughter of an aristocratic family, not only was she interested in literature but also in politics, which provided her with an important role in public life. Thus we see her vanished three times, and each time returning and becoming the center of a refined and intellectual society. Dynamic and vehement, she created the first school for girls in history –where poetry, music and dance were taught–, and by her poems she was known and celebrated throughout the Greek world. The legend that she threw herself off a rock on the island of Lefkada when seeing her love scorned is false. Sappho lived from her writing, she composed epithalamiums for weddings by commission –that sang the nuptial procession– and other poems. But she did not only sing love but also in her verses shows off everything that surrounds her:

> Evening star, you bring together
> that which the morning star scattered,
> you bring the goats,
> you bring the sheep,
> but you do not bring together mother and daughter.
> (50)

These poems, as much as Sappho's fragments, have reached us, and seem enveloped in a steamy aura of water gilded by the sun, or simply water, be that of the River Acheron:

> Hermes, I have invoked you for a long time.
> Nest in my solitude, help me!
> Despot, what death does not arrive by itself alone.
> Nothing brings me joy that can alleviate.
>
> I want to die:
> I want to contemplate the shores of the Acheron,
> flowery lotus, fresh with dew. (50)

These verses reach us like air, that point of humidity belonging to the islands, that of Kos, the fatherland of Hippocrates and of the painter Apelles, and also that of the poet Theocritus. Simonides, considered the "most brilliant of his time", was born in the island of Kea (died in the year 469 B.C.). His marine images still startle us:

> [...] and it overwhelms me
> the roar of the purple sea
> shining around me. (51)

In Delos, the smallest of the Cyclades Islands, Apollo was born, and the maidens participated in the rituals dedicated to this god, singing and dancing. In Naxos, largest of these islands –famous for its marble (from Paros, to the west), and for its wines– another of the great figures, Archilochus, was born. This poet, taking his cue from iambic meter utilized in popular songs, created the iambic trimeter, that would become the classic one for tragedy, and on the other hand, he also utilized dactylic hexameters, trochaic tetrameters and other meters, giving to Greek lyric poetry forms that it would preserve until the end. And in Lesbos, in Mytilene, Alcaeus, a contemporary of Sappho, with whom she shared loves and poems, raised up his voice, and also left the sea forever captured in these lines:

> the wave rolls sometimes from this side
> and sometimes from that; we in the middle
> are carried along on the black ship. (51)

It was Alcaeus who wrote about the poet Sappho: "Oh, crowned in violets, divine / sweet, smiling Sappho" (51). And she, sung and venerated by her contemporaries and in posterity, was admired even by philosophers such as Plato, who manifested: "Some say that the muses are nine. How they are deceived! For here I present the tenth: Sappho of Lesbos" (51). She was the first in utilizing the image of Helen of Troy to express the intensity of love:

> They say that it is a host of riders
> or of princes or boats, the most beautiful
> over the black earth, but I say that it is
> what it is loved.
> It is easy to explain to the whole world

when among the women the most beautiful,
Helena, abandoned
the best of the husbands

and embarked for Troy
without remembering her daughter
or her parents, seduced
by Cypress.
[...]
Because of that she reminds
me of absent Anactoria.
[...]
I would prefer to see her beautiful passage,
and the luminous brilliance of her face,
instead of a troop of Lydians in their carriages
and of armed warriors. (51–52)

Untamed Hair and The Triumphant Ribbon

For a long time Erinna was considered Sappho's disciple, without a doubt because of her way of mentioning her, but the former does not utilize riders nor warriors to express the despair she feels confronted with her dead friend, Baucis, but instead sings her sorrow with her hair untamed in the wind, and evokes games from her childhood. Born in Telos, one of the Sporades islands, it is believed that she studied poetry in Kos, but that she scarcely had time to develop her art: she died at the age of 19, shortly after her friend. Given that, the date of her death is not clear and it does not seem to correlate with the one mentioned in the Souda compilation, which would make her a contemporary of the lyric poet from Lesbos. It is more likely that her life takes place around the year 390 B.C., that is, in the pre-Alexandrine period.

Even though she was not a direct disciple of Sappho, her poems envelop that same luminous aura, at least in the fragments that have reached us from her extensive poem of 300 lines titled "The Spinning Wheel". It is dedicated to Baucis –that beloved companion from infancy– who died on the way to her wedding. The beautiful lines below are enough to capture the height of her art:

> You jumped off the white horse recklessly ...
> and playing like a turtle you crossed the wide patio.
> Unhappy Baucis, I cry when remembering her.
> The traces of those games are still hot,
> and the toys from that time are now embers.
> As little girls we played at brides in bed,
> and at dawn the mother who delivered wool to the maids
> would call you to work at fish salting.
> And what fear the bogeyman gave us when we were little
> with his four legs and big ears
> and always changing appearance.
> But then, dear Baucis, you arrived at the man's bed
> and no longer remembered what you heard as a child in mother's house,
> and Aphrodite lodged oblivion in your mind.
> And now in my lament I cry and renounce,
> for my vulgar feet can no longer leave home,
> nor my eyes see you dead, nor myself lament
> with my hair loose, that the dark shame
> tears apart my cheeks ... (53)

Let us continue among ellipses, even though we may cross to the continent. In it, the women poets tended to be –like Sappho– musicians and choreographers, such as Corinna, Cleobulina, Telesilla, Myrtis o Praxilla. This last one, born in Scion in the 5th Century B.C., was a famous composer of *scolia*, brief fragments that were sung after dinner, and an author of hymns and dithyrambos about mythological and amorous themes. From her hymn to Adonis, there remain three lines –a response to the god of shadows from Hades– where there is allusion to fruits and greens, since all of that is tied to the fertility of nature and, therefore, to the vegetal world:

> Of what I leave behind, the most beautiful is the sun-
> light,
> then, the brilliant stars and the face of the moon,
> and the ripe cucumbers, apples and pears. (53)

These women poets from the continent were situated in the 5th and 6th centuries B.C., and they represent the first impulse of monodic lyric, or that of a single voice. They did not only dominate the metrics but also the themes pertaining to their art, and it is probable that they entoned the hymns from the cult of local divinities, where a soloist, accompanied by a zither or flute, would answer a chorus of girls. They were professionals and they even competed with the men as, according to what tradition says, Myrtis and Corinna did with Pindar. Pausanias recounts having seen in Tanagra, Corinna's homeland, a painting that represented the woman poet placing the triumphant ribbon won in a contest on the forehead of the male poet, which, apparently she succeeded in doing by speaking in the

Boetian dialect, better known by the judges, and also because of her astonishing beauty. Little is left of her poetry, one of the fragments says:

> Terpsichore would tell me
> old love stories to sing
> the white dress of the women of Tanagra
> and of the great enchanted city
> in my voice, a clear swallow ... (54)

In general, nevertheless, and above all in Athens, the female lived entirely reclusively. In fact, in Greece, everything turned around the man, whose complete education required music, writing, mathematics and gymnasium, as much as fighting, swimming and handling of a bow and sling. The female, on the other hand, if she knew how to read and write, that was due to the maternal education, since it was in the home where she learned, above all, to sew, weave and embroider, and she could also play musical instruments and dance. Few ordinary women received a complete education but they did occupy themselves with their own beauty and the use of make-up, perfumes and adornments. It was the prostitutes, courtesans from the upper classes, who were cultured and had economic independence, paid their taxes, carried on an independent life and could attend conferences and even participate in philosophical discussions. These women stood out for their independence, such as Thais or Thargelia, and above all, Diotima and Aspasia, the latter who lived in the 5th Century B.C. and was companion to Pericles – whom she met through Alcibiades– over whom she exercised, apparently, great influence to the point of having attributed to her the origin of the Peloponnesian War.

Centuries later, Plutarch would ask about this matter: "What could this woman have, since she was capable of directing at will the principal men of state and offering to the philosophers the chance to dialogue with her in exalted terms and for long periods of time" (55). She had, it is said, intelligence and oratory capacity; she was a brilliant conversationalist and she shared with Pericles friendships such as Socrates and Anaxagoras.

A public person of great renown, Aspasia was the point of scrutiny from critics, as she was satirized by Aristophanes, but she also appeared in works by Xenophon, Antisthenes, Aeschines, or Plato. According to some, she inspired in the latter the character of Diotima in *The Banquet*, although in *Menexenus* she satirized her relationship with Pericles and attributed to Socrates the irony of saying she was the teacher of many orators. When Pericles died, Aspasia joined up with another important political man, Lisicles, and only his death erases their footprints.

Did Diotima exist, then, in reality? Whether she existed or she was Aspasia's recreation, the fact is that Plato put precisely in her mouth, in dialogue with Socrates, the important definition of love as a "procreation in beauty, as much for the body as for the soul", because a "creative impulse, Socrates, all men have, in fact, not only according to their body but also their soul, and when they meet at a certain age, our nature wants to procreate. But they cannot procreate in things ugly but only in the beautiful ones" (55).

The Freedom of Water

And is this anchoring in beauty not produced due to the contemplation of the sea? From among the waves is born the goddess of Love, Aphrodite, and it seems that, enveloped in its harmonic songs, the modern European woman does the same. On both sides of the Mediterranean, the feminine voice unfolds with force. It is significant that Alexander's grandmother –and Filippo II's mother, called Eurydice– would express her gratitude on a stone tablet: "because the desire of her heart was attended to in prayers, for, being the mother of two adult children, she learned with help letters, inscriptions of words, and to read and write" (56).

After the death of Alexander, in the year 323 B.C., on the other side of the Mediterranean, the opening up of cultural activities takes on a greater momentum. But now since the death of Socrates (in the year 399 B.C.), Greek politics and morality have suffered a change that is reflected in the education of the female, who, beginning from now, has a position that is freer in general and above all in the capitals where the successors of the Macedonian govern. It is really a first step toward their emancipation.

In Tracia, halfway through the 4th Century B.C., there came to attention the first woman philosopher, Hipparchia, who shared her life with Crates, a thinker from the Cynicism Movement. Diogenes Laertius recounts that, her parents being opposed to that union, the thinker, "finally, brought all of his belongings into her presence and said to her: 'Look, this is the husband and these are his belongings; consult with yourself because you won't be able to be my companion without embracing all that is my foundation. ' She chose him right on the moment, and taking on his dress, traveled with Crates, using the marriage publicly, and with both of them attending the ceremonies" (56). And Diogenes goes on to relate an engagement in which Theodorus the Atheist asked her about her abandonment of tasks pertaining to women. She answered him: "Does it seem to you, by chance, that I have not looked after myself in giving my time to the sciences rather than to waste it weaving?" (56).

Above all, even among the cultured women, there were those who loved the quotidian tasks of the simple life, removed from the colorful life of banquets and parties. With freshness they appear in the poetry of Anyte of Tegea, a voice from the Peloponnese, from around 300 B.C. Tegea is situated in Arcadia and the denomination of Arcadia as a bucolic space goes back exactly to the years of Anyte. Very well known outside of her region, even Pausanias talks about this woman poet, telling us that she traveled to Nafpactos to cure a man –sometimes poetry and medicine went together, it was without a doubt a forerunner of the contemporary logotherapy–. Little is known of her life, the only thing definitive are the beautiful couplets of her poems, where forests, meadows, fountains, animals all come to life, the voice of nature and even of the God Pan:

> Sit under the laurel's abundant leaves
> and take a sweet drink from the fountain
> so that your arms and legs tired from the summer's burden
> can rest fanned by the gentle breeze.

Why, rustic Pan, in that dark solitary forest,
are you seated playing the harmonious flute?
So that in the mountains covered with dew
the young calves may graze gathering tender herbs.
(57)

The theme of *locus amoenus* is known in Greece but Anyte brings the novelty of converting nature into interlocutor and introducing a god who speaks in first person. Her poetry is direct and transparent like the fountains she speaks of.

Also around the year 300 B.C. lived Mero de Bizancio, of whom it is known that she wrote elegies and lyric poetry in hexameters. Meleager compared her to Anyte of Tegea, granting her a white lily as a symbolic flower. Her hymn to Poseidon was very famous, but it has not reached us. We are only left with two epigrams that, like Anyte's poems, transfer us to a *locus amoenus*:

Oh save, Hamadryad women, the river virgins
whose ground you tread, divine, with rosy feet.
Protect Cleonymous, who dedicated
these beautiful statues to you,
goddesses, under the pine trees.

You hang a branch from the portico of Aphrodite's temple
full of Dionysius' juice.
Your mother will no longer hold you with loving embrace
nor will she cover you with nectar vines. (57)

In the Magna Grecia colonies, situated to the south of Italy and Sicily, the creations of women flowered equally, for they, according to ancient historians, enjoyed a great deal of freedom. This was translated into an eclosion of women poets such as Nossis of Locri, in whose work are reflected the cults of Aphrodite and Persephone. Her work can be situated around 280 B.C. and it is worth pointing out that in her poems she mentions herself and affirms that she knows Sappho's poetry well, whose name on one occasion she joins with hers. The force with which she affirms her authorship ("This says Nossis") is interesting, as Enheduanna and others had done many years before (58). Meleager, who was the first to gather together a poetic "garland" –let us remember that the word *anthology* primitively meant "branch of flowers"– compares it to the Iris flower.

Nossis achieved such fame among her fellow citizens and she was given numerous tasks, like writing couplets to accompany a civic ex-voto, perhaps the only occasion in her poems in which men appear as agile and valiant, fending off an attack and chasing away the enemy:

> From their shoulders the Bretios threw down
> their arms, wounded at the hands of the agile Locrios.
> As a hymn to their courage they lie in the temple
> of the gods and do not long for the cowardly arms they
> left behind. (58)

Nossis was also the author of numerous epigrams, like the one dedicated to Sappho or destined for Rinton's tomb:

> Pass by after a healthy laugh
> and a kind word. I am Rinton of Syracuse,

> the small nightingale of the Muses. With the tragic parodies
> I gathered my own ivy. (58)

Likewise, she wrote these lines in which she praises Sabastide:

> One can tell from far away that it is Sabastide,
> that portrait, for its form and its nobility.
> Look at it, discover in it its prudence and its sweetness.
> May you enjoy it, happy woman. (58)

A LIGHT BEYOND

It was above all in Alexandria that the bloom of emancipation of woman became a slender stem and then flowered, but was also cut down. One must not forget that in that city there was born a mythical character, but at the same time also real, as interesting and complex as Cleopatra VII. Previously, in the 3rd Century B.C., Arsinoe, daughter of Ptolemy I and Berenice, had stood out likewise for her political gifts and her daring. Married at 17 to Lysimachus, King of Tracia, upon becoming a widow she returned to Egypt where her brother Ptolemy II reigned. She was able to achieve that his wife be exiled, married him and devoted herself to governing, turning Alexandria into a great economic capital.

As for CleopatraVII, E. M. Forster describes her this way: "Although passionate, she was not a slave of passion, and even less of sentimentalism. What was important to her was her security, as well as the security of Egypt" (59). Examined through this prism, the English author describes her movements as children of a cold intelligence and open to employing all resources.

Again it was the sea and the proximity of the East. In Alexandria, with the Ptolemys, philosophy and science gained much momentum. There was born Neoplatonism, when Plotinus returned, after having joined an expedition to fight against Persia for the purposes of getting to know Zoroastrianism, Buddhism and Hinduism closely. That tremendous intellectual restlessness, on behalf of the city, was represented by the famous lighthouse, from whose third floor, thanks to a mysterious "mirror", boats could be seen in the distance, invisible at first sight. Next to the lighthouse, and they were significant, were the Museion –constructed in imitation of the one in Athens– and the Library –that ended up possessing five hundred thousand books– unfortunately destroyed by the fire in times of Cesar. His Serapis temple was the last bastion of Paganism against Christianity.

Connected to the capital of the Ptolemais are found the names Euclid, Eratosthenes, Erasistratus, in science, but also those of Clement of Alexandria, Origen, Arius or Athanasius. Already in the 5th Century, Hypatia's name stands out –disciple of Porphyrion, a philosopher, mathematician, and knowledgeable about the physics and astronomy of her time– she was the last follower of the doctrines of Plato and Plotinus. She taught in the Museion at the moment when Christianity became obligatory and pagans were being pursued. One day, when she was on her way to give classes, Cirillo's army detained her, took her to the Cesareum and there a mob of Christians stoned her to death. And then began obscurantism and intolerance.

Socrates of Constantinople said of her: "She achieved such a level of culture that she was greatly superior to contemporary philosophers. Heir of the Neoplatonic School of Plotinus, she would explain all of the philosophical sciences to whomever desired. For this reason, whoever wanted to think philosophically would come from anywhere to wherever she was" (60). Among her works is notice of a commentary on Diophantus of Alexandria's *Arithmetic*, and another of Apollonius of Perga's *Conic Sections*. She also carried out a revision of Claudius Ptolemy's *Astronomical Tables*, and the edition of the commentary to Euclid's *Elements*. She invented a distiller and an artifact to measure the level of water, and a hydrometer to calculate the weight of the liquids, a precursor of the contemporary aerometer.

Hypatia died in the year 415 or 416, historians cannot agree on the date. In times of Justinian, there was an attempt to counterbalance her stature juxtaposing her with that of Saint Catherine of Alexandria, to whom a monastery in the Sinai was dedicated.

Rome, a Circle In a Square

Nothing –not even fragments– have remained to us from the writings of Hypatia; we know about them from her disciples Synesius of Cyrenaica or Hesychius of Alexandria, the Hebrew one. This fact could be explained by the so extensive religious persecution. It does not make sense, on the other hand, that Roman women writers are hardly noted, and that we are only left with two fragments from Cornelia's letters, the summary of an eloquent speech by Hortensia and six poems from Sulpitia. Given everything, according to some scholars, like Linda Fierz-David, it was in Rome where the European woman was truly given shape.

The wave of sensibility toward culture that originated in the islands and the Greek colonies was expanding and modified on the Italian peninsula, deriving from a different education focus. The Roman female children from wealthy families would go to school, with the boys, until age 12, and afterwards, if the husband or father authorized it, would continue studying with tutors who taught them the Classics. It was common that they would learn to sing, dance and play an instrument. At age 12, marriage could be granted, even though these girls were not considered adults until age 14. From that point on, they remained shut in the house, given to spinning with a wheel and a spindle, and they were called "madam". Their relationship with men, the father to whom they owed their education and freedom, the tutor –master and friend– and the rest, in general, was more like companionship than submissiveness.

The levels of autonomy that women achieved in this society are notable, even for a brief period of time. Those who had assets –shoed and dressed by slaves and always accompanied by one of them– enjoyed relative freedom. They had to be discreet, and therefore only showed themselves in public when covered by a veil, and to accept the husband as master, just as he was of the servants. The day after the wedding, the brides were considered "matrons", and from that moment on were not allowed to drink wine or abort without their husband's permission. Nevertheless, they participated in the social life of the home, and, when they went out shopping, on the street, the way was opened up for them; they would attend public spectacles; they accompanied their husbands to banquets and they advised them in their decisions. They could also interview in criminal causes or as plaintiffs or witnesses. And, if the moment arrived, they had the right to request a divorce and, in addition, to retain part of the inheritance. When they became widowed, they were free and had a fortune at their disposal.

On the other hand, matrimony could take place *ad manus* or *sine manus*, in the first case the husband had all the power over his wife; in the second, she continued to belong to her family of origin. And there also existed licit free unions: the concubinage, the matrimony *sine connubio* (without union), when one of the members of the couple did not have Roman citizenship, and the *contuvernio,* the marital life between slaves. The marital bond could be dissolved by the death of one of the spouses, loss of citizenship, captivity, disappearance or deportation, and divorce. This last one was achieved by mutual agreement, a repudiation of one of the parties, or impotence. When it was due to dishonorable conduct on the part of the husband, the wife would retain custody of the children.

There were moments of greater liberty for Roman women: during the Bacchic cults, the Bacchanalia. Then they could drink wine and practice sex openly. Given everything, the Senate considered these festivals to be scandalous and prohibited them in the year 186 B.C. During that time there existed a corporation of very influential women, the *conventus matronarum* ("an assembly of married women") with religious purposes, whose meeting place was located in Trajan's forum.

Now then, these steps toward future liberties lasted little time. In that *Square Rome ("Roma quadrata")*, the circle (achieved by the groove of Romulo's plow) in the square was only a passing achievement. The advances disappeared with the arrival of Augustus, who imposed some rigorous laws. Aulus Gellius, in the 2nd Century, wrote: "If you surprise a woman in adultery, you can kill her with impunity without bringing any judgment; but if she surprised you in any conjugal infidelity, she would not dare, nor does she have any right to move a finger against you" (63). And Tacitus (55?-120?), in his *Annals*, remembered that terrible law that prohibited killing a virgin[3]: "The historians of the period relate that, as it was considered unheard of that a virgin would suffer a capital punishment, the executioner would rape her just as he was putting a rope around her neck" (63).

3 Still in force, and with the same consequence, among Islamic peoples.

The period of light came about, above all, at the end of the Republican era and the beginning of the Empire. Despite its brevity, it was reflected in art, science, philosophy and literature. But around the names of Roman women artists, there are nothing but broken angles and blurry spaces. But Iaia of Cyzicus, around the year 100 B.C. –says Pliny– "used the painting brush as much as the marble chisel" (63), that Pamphylia, in times of Nero, wrote a *Historic Miscellany*, that Beruria of Jerusalem lived in the 2nd Century…

Linda Fierz-David, in her book, the *Villa of the Mysteries Pompeii*, points out that on the walls of said villa there are paintings where some women appear eating comfortably and others in Dionysian scenes. The cornerstone of the house, she affirms, was a statue of Livia, the empress, wife of Augustus, and who incarnated a "cultural conviction and a political program" and it "represented the Roman tradition and the European values developed in Rome, that reached their apogee once Rome had absorbed all of its Greek heritage", in the last centuries of the Republic. The author insists: "It was not Greece, but Rome –the Rome of the Republic clearly– the cradle of the European woman as a natural product and bearer of that same culture. Even if it is true that customs were very different". And she refers in her support of Guglielmo Ferrero (*The Women of the Caesars*), according to whom "the equality between women and men, that we claim to be our supreme objective, was achieved first by the women of Rome" (63).

Given everything, the same Fierz-David advises us: "The

image incarnated by Livia appears to us to be in some way incomplete, given that the ethical and conscious perception of maternity was absent in the Roman female. This notion was developed for the first time in the Christian world" (63). Now then, it could be, in effect, that Christianity insisted on that concept but, for example, by the references that Latin writers give us of Cornelia, and from the fragments of her letters that remain, it can be deduced justly that this notorious woman was a model of mother and spouse; not in vain was she known as "Cornelia, the mother of the Gracchi". Daughter of Publius Cornelius Scipio Africanus, and married to Tiberius Sempronius Gracchus, she had 12 children (only three survived), of whose education she took charge. Cicero, referring to the importance of hearing during childhood, wrote exactly: "It is important whom one hears daily at home, with whom she/he speaks as a child, how the parents and the pedagogues speak, and even the mothers. We can read the letters of Cornelia, mother of the Gracchi: In them one sees children educated not only in their mother's laps but also in the manner of speaking" (63-64). Quintilian mentions her when he refers to this point: "We know that the elegance of the Gracchi was due in great part to their mother, Cornelia, whose very cultured language has been preserved for posterity in some epistles" (64). Reading the fragments mentioned, we realize that Cornelia was intelligent and daring, because of the audacious pieces of advice that she gives to her son Gayo, even at the risk of being misinterpreted.

Once again, the importance of the family question remains primary, essential, above all, to the education of the female.

Hortensia, as Valerius Maximus tell us, "revived the art of her father", Quintus Hortensius Hortalus (64). She did it in a famous speech that was published, and then later summarized by Apian in his *Roman History*. Apparently, the orator, a "great Republican leader" (Ronald Syme), was married to Quintus Servelious Cepion, adoptive father of Marcus Brutus. In the year 42 B.C., she was opposed to a tax threatening to be imposed on the richest women of the city, since they (these women), would have favored lending economic help in the event of a war against foreign peoples but not for a civil war. Thus, as spokesperson for the *Order of Ladies*, she pronounced her celebrated speech in the Roman Forum, and whose clarity and expository efficiency we can capture by means of a simple fragment from Apian's *History*:

> Why do we have to pay taxes if we do not have any participation in the judiciary, in commendations, in the generalship, no, not at all, in the government of public matters, in which you embroil yourselves in personal fights that end up in such great calamities? Why do you say that we are at war? When the women have contributed with taxes? For these (women), their own natural condition exempts them from it throughout humanity, and our mothers, above and beyond their own essence as women contributed their taxes on occasion, and for once, when you were in danger of losing the whole empire, and even the same city, under the Carthaginian assault. But then they made a voluntary contribution, and not at the expense of their lands or fields, or dowries, or homes, without which life can be impossible for free women, not only with their personal jewels, without these ever having been subjected to taxation, nor under the fear of

> traitors or accusers, nor under bribery. And besides, what fear do you have now for the empire or the countryland? Most certainly war against the Gauls or the Parthians will come and we will not be inferior to our mothers in contributing to its salvation, but for civil fights we would never bring anything nor would we help you fight some against the others. Nor did we do it in the time of Cesar or Pompeii, nor did Mario nor Cinna oblige us to do so, not even Silla, who exercised absolute power over the country, and you all affirm that you are consolidating the Republic. (64-65)

In truth, there were reasons that Hortensia's speech became renowned. Without a doubt she had become familiar with this type of pronouncement since childhood, but it still continued to surprise Valerius Maximus that it was she, and not her brothers, who had developed the paternal gift.

The poet Sulpicia also belonged to a family of name, that moved in the intellectual world of the moment. After the death of her father, Servius Sulpicio Rufus, her uncle, Marcus Valerius Mesalla, was her tutor and to him she refers in one of those six poems of hers rescued from the jaws of time. This small sample of her writing, that dates from the first half of the 1st Century B.C., collected in Book III of Tibulus' poetic work, follows the manner of the period (Catulus, Ovid) and one could say that it is a mere fruit of circumstances. Thus reach us the desires of a young girl –she calls herself *puella* ("the girl")– enamored of a young man whom she calls Cerinthus, that (as her translator Aurora López points out) are centered on "love, modesty and fame" (65). The poetry lines also denote moments of rebellion when confronted with the veleities of the beloved, which is expressed with great naturalness. I quote below the only sample we have of a female woman poet:

> Love reached me finally, and it is such that to hide it from modesty
> before baring it to someone, might give me a worse reputation.
> Cytherea, overcome by the requests of the water nymphs, [4]
> brought it to me and left it on my lap.
> Venus fulfilled her promise: may that person
> who had not shared her own, retell my joys.
> I would not want to trust anything to sealed splints,
> so that no one reads them before my love,
> but it enchants me to work against the norm, to pretend for appearance
> angers me: we were each of us worthy of the other, let them say that.
>
> Boringly the birthday approaches, for sadly I will have to spend
> it in the annoying field, and without Cerinthus.
> Is there anything more pleasing than the city? Is a house in the country
> and the cold river of Arezzo an appropriate place for a girl?
> Rest for once, Messala, worried too much for me;
> at times, kindred, travels are not opportune.
> You carry me away, but here I leave the soul and senses

4 Acquatic nymphs

by my own decision, even though you might not allow it.

Do you know that the inopportune trip no longer worries your beloved?
I can now be in Rome for your birthday.
We shall celebrate together the great day of your anniversary
that comes by chance, when you least expected.

What you allow yourself is pretty, not concerning yourself for me,
assured that I am going to fall suddenly like a foolish woman.
May it be yours the preoccupation for the toga and the pelt of she who wears it,
burdened with her basket, before Sulpicia, daughter of Servius.
For me, let them worry those who have care as their main motive,
that I am not going to sleep with just anyone.

Do you have, Cerinthus, a devout preoccupation for your beloved,
because now the fever mistreats my tired body?
Ay! I would not want to free myself from the sorrowful sickness,
if I did not think that you also want it.
But, what would it be worth to me to be free from this sickness,
If you can endure my ills with an indifferent heart?

For you, may it not be me, light of mine, a burning anxiety
which seems how I was some days ago,

if I made some mistake, foolish in my excess of youth,
of which I confess that I regret more,
is having left you alone yesterday night
wanting to dissimulate my burning passion. (65-67)

There are no ellipses, in this case, but surrounding the poem is an abysmal sea of absence of women's voices that were expressed in Rome and in Latin. They are, then, Sulpicia's poems, and with them the two fragments from Cornelia's letters and the summary of Hortensia's speech, like islands in that literary sea, whose waves rise to the heights of a Virgil, a Catullus, or an Ovid.

Bibliography

Anglada, M. A., *Les germanes de Safo (The Sapphire Sisters)*, Antologie de poètes hellénistiques, Edhasa, Barcelona, 1983.

Durant, W. *La vida de Grecia* (*The life of Greece*). Editorial Sudamericana, Buenos Aires, 1945.

Dzielska, M. *Hipatía de Alejandría (Hypatia of Alexandria)*, Siruela, Madrid, 2003.

Fierz–David, L. *La villa de los misterios de Pompeya (The Villa of Mysteries in Pompeii)*, Atalanta, Girona, 2005.

Forster, E. M., *Alejandría* (*Alexandria*), Seix Barral, Barcelona, 1984.

Jiménez, L., "Alejandrinas" ("Alexandrines") in *Biblioteca Alejandrina. Homenaje a la Memoria, apuesta por el futuro (Alexandrine Library: Homage to Memory, Bet on the Future)*, Biblioteca Nacional, Madrid, 2003, pp. 81–92.

López, A., "*Cartas* de Cornelia y *Elegías* de Sulpicia" ("Cornelia's *Letters* and Sulpicia's *Elegies*"), in *Grecia y Roma II, Lecturas pendientes* (*Greece and Rome II, Pending Readings*), Ed. of A. Pociña Pérez and J. García González, Ed. University of Granada, 2008.

López, A. *De Safo a Alfonsina. Mujeres en su literatura y en la masculina. (From Sappho to Alfonsina. Women in their Literature and in Men's),* Arcibel Editors, Sevilla, 2008.

Muller, C. O. *Historia de la literatura griega* (*History of Greek Literature*), Editorial Americalee, Buenos Aires, 1946.

Quasimodo, S. *Lirici greci* (*Greek Lyric*), Mondadori, Verona, 1960.

Sappho, *Poemas y fragmentos (Poems and Fragments)*, Hiperion, Madrid, 1990.

__________. *Safo y sus discípulas, poemas (Sappho and her Disciples, Poems*), Ediciones del Oriente y del Mediterráneo, Guadarrama, 2009.

Transcelan, B., *Poemas de Alejandría. El ángel y el cisne (Poems of Alexandria. The Angel and the Swan)*, introduction C. Janés, *La ciudad y el enigma (The City and the Enigma)*, adamaRamada, Madrid, 2008.

Trypanis, C. A. *Greek Poetry. From Homer to Seferis*, Faber & Faber, London and Boston, 1981.

IV- Closed Gardens; Open Pleasures: Arab-Andalusian Women Poets

When in the desert an oasis surges up, no matter how arid, the flavor of its fruits is incomparable. The date of Haudrimont ignites the veins, that when fused with minimal freshness –which will not be less than 30 degrees–, and that brings the decline of the afternoon, it inspires men and women to sing and dance in a celebration of life. And it is the woman who directs the dance and goes around inviting, everyone who is present, to come up on the dais and become involved in the dance, and she is also the one, in general, who sings.

The joy of being alive in the desert is branched off in the joy of the senses and it emerges in the evocative voice of perfumes and flavors, light from the stars and lightness of water. These elements are not lost but instead seem to be intensified, when the Conquest brings to the Arab people lands with gardens and pools, where the palm tree can cohabit with the rose, the orange blossom, and the pomegranate. The bases are consolidated and the euphoria multiplies on passing from the Arabian peninsula to Syria (Damascus), to Iraq (the Tigris and Euphrates), to Egypt (the Nile), and to Spain.

In the different stages of their expansion, the Arab people begin integrating some of the fundamental elements of the culture of the place, such as the Greek, the Roman, not to mention the Jewish –it is known that the Koran derives from the Bible–. Of course these movements do not always stand out immediately, but the fact is that through the work of art is manifested, on one hand, that which is present and, on the other hand, that which is intuited or divined. At times, nevertheless, not only the first substrates, but the art itself, can remain in obscurity and then emerge into the light at a determined moment. This has happened with the lyric writing of the Andalusian women poets, whose rebirth is presented as something open.

Virginia Woolf, in her work *A Room of Her Own*, spoke of the infinite obstacles that woman encounters at the moment of writing, and of how certain "external" circumstances influence her concrete creativity. Expanding the concept of "circumstances" and taking it to the limits of "historical moment", it becomes clear that women's writing is produced in periods when the society invites it, by its way of incorporating the female –this is the case of the first great novelist, Murasaki Shikibu– even though, on the other hand, the education possibilities granted her by her family level were also influential. On other occasions, the determining factor is, above all, the opening up of customs. So it is that we have seen that in the Greek Islands, in the 4th Century B.C., the work of Sappho is born, and is still influential in universal literature.

Caravan Of Stories

After the fall of the Roman Empire, after the invasion of the Barbarians and the ferocious battles that lasted for several centuries, the brutality began to disappear slowly and some modifications were begun. There could be, for example, the sudden flowering of the troubadours in the courts of the south of France, closely connected to the change undergoing the focus on the love sentiment, not distant from the influence of the Arab world and through it, Platonism.

Asín Palacios, in the *Muslim Eschatology of the Divine Comedy*, exposed how, with the Arabs, the concept of *udri* love, which exalted and idealized the female, gained diffusion and spread not only throughout all of Spain but also to France and to Italy where, with the passing of time, it led literarily to the *dolce stil nuovo* thanks to Brunetto Latini, Dante's teacher, an ambassador in the court of Alfonso The Wise.

Regarding Udri love, García Gómez, in his preliminary study of the work of Ibn Hazm, *The Dove's Necklace*, says that it was a myth created by the Eastern rhetoricians, "concretely by poets such as Urwa, Kutayu, Majnun and above all Chanil, who were dying from love, heroes of a refined idealism and practitioners of an ambiguous chastity, whose erotic north was a morbid perpetuation of desire" (71). This myth, that goes back to the 7th Century, with the work of Layla and Majnun, of the Persian Nizami, and, above all, with the much later version of the

Turk Fuzuli[5], achieved its most beautiful literary expression. The legend of those two lovers was assimilated into the Platonic theories in Baghdad at the end of the 9th Century by Ibn Dawud, in his *Book of the Flower*, that dates from the year 890, a work that arrived relatively early to Córdoba. Some 70 years later, during the Caliphate of Al Hakam II al-Mustansir bi-llan (961-976), the writer Jaén Ahmad ibn Farah collected an anthology of Arab-Andalusian poets who imitated him, with the title *The Book of the Orchards*. This takes place in the 10th Century, at the end of which Ibn Hazm was born, the maximum representative of this literature.

In the same period, that is in the 10th Century, but very removed from the Udri love, Arab-Andalusian women poets come into being, whose appearance is like a striking and exotic flower from those "orchards", as much for how accomplished their art was as for its tone of complete abandonment. In fact, these women creators, distant from any Platonism, show off an expressive freedom whose origin seems to be at the margins of what their social position and education could grant, and even the same fashion in Baghdad. When before had a woman written a poem like that which is titled "To a lover to whom I send peaches"? Muhya bint Al-Tayanni o al Qurtubiyya did it in the 11th Century:

> Oh, you who gives peaches to your beloved,
> welcome that fruit that gladdens the souls!
> Its roundness imitates the breast of the maidens
> but the head humiliates that of the penises. (71)

5 In Spain we know her thanks to the translation of Solimán Salom, *Leyla and Mecnun*, Editora Nacional, Madrid, 1982.

The fruit has cleverly transformed itself and, in that way, speaks to us of more than just freedom in the social sphere. It has to do with an interior freedom and a different vision of things, that Western woman, until today, has never enjoyed, and also of a literary tradition with a Middle Eastern backdrop. I refer to the *Thousand and One Nights*, transmitted orally, whose first nucleus was collected in the Persian book *One Thousand Stories*.

By means of travel analogous to the caravans, which were following the silk route, mouth to mouth, they were spreading these stories throughout the Islamic world, forming a substratum of marked emphasis on the erotic aspect of the love relationships, that explains, among other things, at least, the tone of the poetry of the Arab-Andalusian poets. The already mentioned stories, the oldest of which were already known in the the 17th Century, originated in the tradition of Persia, Iraq, Afghanistan, Uzbekistan and India. Those originating in China and Egypt were added later, and together they were edited for the first time in the Arabic language in the 11th Century. Later they would be completed by the linking of all of them through the figure of Scheherezade and with the story of Simbad the sailor.

The powerful oral tradition –that oscillates between the aridity of the desert and the juiciest of fruits– opened up, without a doubt, the possibilities of the open use of eroticism within the literature of the countries under Arab control, which is reflected even in some of the Sufi texts, like Rumi's *Masnavi*. This factor is not to be scorned, as it is added to the way of life of the Arab-Andalusian women, in whose songs the confluence of the exotic oases with the gardens and patios of Spain was likely determinant.

The great scholars, at any rate, insist on the multiple possibilities that the Andalusian women had at their reach, in comparison with their contemporaries, both Christian and Muslim from the East. Thus, Adolf Friedrich von Schack affirms: "The situation of women in Spain was freer than among the other Muslim peoples. Women would take part in the entire intellectual climate of their time, and the number of those who achieved fame for their scientific achievements or disputing poetry prizes with men was high. Such a sophisticated civilization was the reason that they were taxed in Spain an amount that the Muslim East had never taxed them" (72-73). Luis Gonzalvo y París says: "We cannot see in their poetry but one of many courses open in that society to the initiatives of women, whose education was not essentially different from that which men received" (73).

Mahmoud Sobh insists that women *hara'ir* (free, noble) participated in culture camps, taught letters and even had other professions, including Medicine, in the East. For his part, Henri Peres, in *Splendor of Al-Andal*us, talks about the freedom of movement of the young Andalusian woman (despite being veiled and, at certain meetings, would sing hidden by a curtain), giving concrete examples, like the one of the poet Al Ramadi who, strolling one Friday in the garden of the Banu Marwan of Córdoba, takes up conversation with a young woman and does not leave her before obtaining a date for the following Friday. He also affirms that some of the Andalusian women poets were "juris consults, others were ascetics, a large part of them transcribers of the Koran", up to the end of the 10th Century, while "in the 11th Century –says Peres– the woman tends to occupy a position at the forefront of society, (and) the flowering of love poetry, that makes her an idealized adult being, shows us that, even if still confined in the gynaeceum, although enjoying a relative freedom, the Andalusian woman feels almost equal to the male, and claims, like him, the right to life" (73).

The Body As A Goal

This would not explain, however, the tone of some of their poems since, in the literary terrain, the Provençal female troubadours boasted the same equality and their style is very different. Perhaps the difference between the Arab-Andalusian women poets and other women poets of the period is rooted in their different concept of the treatment between man and woman. In this respect not only is the life of the harem fundamental, but also the importance of the female slave singers and dancers in relation to the world of pleasure. These women also received a rigorous education. In a "kind of academies-conservatories, the most eclectic teachings and the most varied artistic knowledge were taught to the slave musicians and dancers", says Peres (74). There they learned logic, geometry, astrolabe, astronomy, grammar, prose, "belles lettres", and calligraphy. And they learned, above all, grace and charm.

Among these schools was the one that existed in Córdoba. Ibn Bassam referring to a woman singer who finished there, said: "Nobody saw, in that period, a woman with a more graceful style, more agile movements, such a fine silhouette, the sweetest voice, knowing how to sing better, more outstanding in the art of writing, in calligraphy, a more refined culture, a purer diction; she did not commit a single dialectal error in what she wrote or sang, so great was her knowledge of morphology, lexicography and metrics; she even knew of medicine, natural history and anatomy, and other sciences in which the wise men of the time would have been found inferior. She stood out in the handling of arms ("tiqaf"), in the flipping of leather shields, in the juggling games with sables, lances and sharp daggers; in everything she had no match, not equal or equivalent" (74).

The goal of these teachings was, then, the art of seduction in all aspects, and in a manner that disregarded caution. Peres also says: "A passage from Ibn Jaldun's *Prolegomenon* shows us that the dancers would hang little horses ('kurray') from their suits, called 'qaba,' to represent the riders that rushed to the attack, who battled as they retreated and who returned to combat. These 'qaba' must have been, judging by the poets' descriptions, tunic garments that could be opened completely from top to bottom to suddenly allow the appearance of the nude 'like a flower bud opening up, ' as Al-Mu'tamid says" (74).

The Arab-Andalusian female, therefore, necessarily had a concept of the body that was very different from the one held by the Christian female, for whom it was fundamentally a basis of sin. It did not have only to do with, therefore, the intellectual possibilities to be able to participate in a literature that revolves around the sensual, but also with a real awareness of pleasure and of the place that sex occupied in it. On the other hand, that which in appearance could be understood as limitation, the use of the veil or life in the harem, could in reality not be that. The Arab woman, who lives surrounded by other women, is one among other spouses, who sees the husband at the hour of meals or in bed, does not find herself continually under the eyes of the male judge, nor does she need to protect herself with her modesty from the rest of the men. In the harem she thinks and expresses herself freely and the theme of sex is, without a doubt, one of the more habitual ones, so common that its name is attached to many things.

All of this should not induce us to think that the creativity of the Arab-Andalusian women is limited to themes of love, even though these dominate. Satire, the laudatory poem, even erudite or religious poetry, are included in her production. We do not know, nevertheless, to what extent what we can access is representative, since nobody took charge of collecting her works, and we owe to fate that which remains, generally included in epistolaries or biographies of known authors.

Missives and Wrongs

It is clear, nevertheless, that the style of the Arab-Andalusian women is very alive; that they write with naturalness, following the Eastern customs, without limiting poetry to a passive song, but instead they grant it an immediate and dynamic usefulness: to complete some proposed lines, to participate in a common work, to answer a missive or a wrong, etc.. For that reason it is not surprising that such creativity stands out for the freshness of its language, and an abandon that on occasion could be confused with insolence.

The oldest poem that remains from the first known Arab-Andalusian woman poet, Hassana Al-Tamimiya, whose birthdate is situated during the emirate of Abderramán I (756-788), is laudatory. This poet appears to us as a resolute woman and capable of defending herself for herself. Her verses are dedicated to the emir Al Hakam I, from whom she sought protection. In reality that which is known about Hassana is very little, but yes that she lived in Elvira (Granada) and that she had problems with its governor, for which she would frequently seek out the emir, then Abderramán II, to whom she dedicated a poem as well, that says:

> Toward the master of generosity and glory my mounts have advanced,
> crossing the distances, ignited by the fire of the sun and of noon,
> I come to him, for he is the best restorative, so that he can repair my bankruptcies,
> and repair me from the tyrant Yábir.

I, and my orphaned brothers and sisters, we are at the mercy of his hands
like the little bird that finds itself between the claws of an eagle.
Well do I deserve it to be said that I am desolate,
by the death of Abu-Asi who was my protector.
May the rain water him! If he were alive, the ferocious fate
would not have delivered me to the ferocity of a powerful man.
Would Yábir be able to erase what the hand of Al-Hakam wrote?
Then a great evil will be committed with my goods. (76)

This has to do with a poem that is intelligently constructed, not of a coarse stammer. Already in the 9th Century there is, then, in Spain a perfectly formed feminine voice.

Among the known Arab-Andalusian women poets, the majority were either born or lived in Córdoba, Sevilla or Granada, cities celebrated for their gardens. But also from Almería there reaches us that atmosphere propitious for lyric poetry, from the few verses we know from Al– Gassaniyya. They are dedicated to the Prince Jayran Al-Amiri, to whom she feels herself joined, as if speaking of two branches:

To live was a delicacy, and the garden
of life, radiant and perfumed.
Happy nights when I did not fear
reproaches from the one I loved,
nor did the abandon of being together frighten me,
in this pleasure that assaulted us

and we embraced the desires
like the branches that embrace each other pushed by the wind. (76)

Two of the most daring Arab-Andalusian women poets were born in Córdoba, the princess Wallada and her disciple, already mentioned, Muhya Bint al Tayyani o Al Qurtubiyya. Wallada, daughter of the Caliph Muhammed III al-Mustakfi, who occupied the throne only 17 months between 1024-1025, was a cultured and brilliant woman, capable of competing with and of surpassing the male poets of the period. Her great gifts allowed her to synthesize two concepts in one line, thanks to an image, as in these, written on passing before the door of Ibn Abdus, drenched in rain:

You are the generous one and this pool is Egypt
overflowing, the two of you together are the sea. (77)

Wallada inspired in the celebrated Cordoban poet Ibn Zaydun his most beautiful love poems, and she dedicated some beautiful lines to him, within the classical Arabic tradition of the time, the same subtlety of suggestions, at times evoking the enveloping night:

When the night falls, await my visit,
for I see that the night is what best covers up secrets;
I feel a love for you that if the stars felt it
the sun would not shine,
nor would the moon come out, and the stars
would not begin their nocturnal journey. (77)

A very different tone, nevertheless, characterizes the violent satire that she directed to the same poet, angered by his dalliances with a black slave:

> Your nickname is the hexagon, an epithet
> that will not leave you
> not even after life leaves you:
> pederast, damn adulterer,
> bastard, cuckold and thief. (77)

In the same style is the poem that Muhya bint Al-Tayanni al-Qurtubiyya wrote expressly against her teacher and protector Wallada. Muya, daughter of a fig merchant, had, without doubt, access to the rooms reserved for the princess in order to deliver the figs. Wallada noticed her and took charge of seeing that she received an education. It is not known what motives Muya had to satirize her (Wallada) in verses where she alludes to a passage from the Koran that represents the pregnant Virgin leaning on a palm tree that by divine inclination drops fresh and ripe dates on her:

> Wallada gave birth and has no husband,
> the secret is revealed,
> she has imitated Mary
> but the palm tree that the Virgin would shake
> for Wallada is an erect penis. (78)

In my judgment this is one of the key poems of the lyric writing of these women, since in it one can see clearly that it has been written with the purpose of indicting the male, but that it responds instead to the abandon and freedom of expression on the part of women in the harem. This seems to contradict the refined education that the slaves received, but it is probably not so; in all likelihood this responded to certain indications from the Koran where it refers to the *uríes* (Uris), and affirms that with them one should never speak of "frivolous" things.

Safe From Thirst

From a slave poet, the Cordobesa Mut'a, only one delightful poem remains to us. Her master was the celebrated musician Ziryab, and she, with frequency, would sing or serve the drinks in the meetings presided over by Abderramán II. Understanding that she was pleasing to him, she declared her love singing some verses and thus revealing the secret. Ziryab, upon realizing, gifted her to the emir. In the poem, Mut'a gives Abderramán the title of "quarsi", demonym of the Quarish tribe, from which the Omeyas came originally:

> Oh you, who hide your passion,
> who can hide the day?
> I had a heart,
> but I fell in love and it flew away,
> woe is me, was it mine or loaned?
> I love a "quarsi"
> and for him I have forgotten shame. (79)

If this poem by Mut'a enclosed some indirect message, the famous and only poem that remains from Butayna, it is directly a missive. In fact, these verses are so anchored in daily life that we feel them as small narrations, resonating profoundly that caravan of stories, not necessarily erotic. Butayna, daughter of the King Mutamid, reflected in those verses her history full of adventures: with the sacking of the palace, she was carried off as a captive and then sold as a concubine to a businessman from Seville, who then gave her to his son. She prevented those actions from being consummated taking refuge in her lineage and demanding a marriage contract, if her father consented. For this reason she sent these verses written by her own hand and letter to the king:

Listen to my speech and attend to my words,
for behavior shows who is noble.
You do not know that I was captured, but neither
that I am the daughter of a king descended from the Abbadíes,
a great king whose time has gone
–thus does time make its way toward ruin!–.
When God wished to separate us
and made us try, as a travel fee,
the taste of sadness,
hypocrisy rose up
against my father and his own kingdom,
and the separation, that nobody wanted, came nearer.
I left fleeing,
a man overpowered me
and, in his behavior, did not behave correctly,
because he sold me as they would sell the slaves;
but he has joined me with someone who protects me from everything,
except adversity, and he wants me
to marry his virgin son,
entrepreneur, of good character,
who goes to you to ask your opinion to satisfy you
–now you see the integrity of my conduct–.
Oh how I hope, father of mine, that you inform me
if he can expect my affection,
and I hope Rumaykiyya, the queen, with her favor,
will ask for prosperity and happiness on our behalf.
(79-80)

When Al-Mutamid, then jailed in Agmat, received this missive, it filled him with joy, since it gave him notice that Butayna was still alive, and he sent her the matrimonial contract with this response:

> Dear daughter, be affectionate with him,
> time has decreed that you accept him. (80)

The verses of Butayna became known in all of the Occidental West. It has to do with, nevertheless, a descriptive poem, oriented toward a concrete end, a poem, fundamentally, efficient.

It also achieves a goal, very different on the other hand, the only one we know of Ibnat ibn al- Sakkan, a Málaga woman of whom we only know that she lived until old age and spent time with writers from the period. It is enough, nevertheless, to see her extraordinary talent, with the anecdote and poem included, collected by Abu Bakr Muhammed Ibu Yahya al Suli, according to whom, finding himself with her in a meeting, a crow passed over and someone asked her to describe it. She answered, improvising:

> Close by us has passed a crow,
> wiping the face of the hills,
> and I have said to it: Be welcome,
> color of the hair of youth. (80)

The most famous of the Hispanic-Arab women poets, and that of whom more poems are preserved, was, nevertheless, Hafsa bint al-Hayy al-Rakuniyya, who, apparently, at the end of her life occupied herself with the education of the Almohad princesses in the palace of Yakub al-Mansour in Marrakesh, where she died in 1191. Her beauty unleased stormy passions, even indirectly causing the death of the poet Abu Yafar, crucified by the order of Abu Said Utman, governor of Granada, enamored of her as was the former. Teresa Garulo, en el *Diwan de las poetisas de Al-Andalus* (*Divan of the Andalusian Women Poets*), collects some verses written by him after having spent an afternoon with the woman poet in the garden of the famous Hawr Mu'ammal of Granada:

> May God protect a night that he spent without reprobation
> and he hid us in Hawr Mu'ammal!
> An aroma from Nayd was throbbing
> that, on blowing, shook with the smell of carnations,
> a turtledove cooed in the trees,
> and the branches of the myrtles leaned over the creek
> and the garden seemed exhilarated
> by what it witnessed:
> embraces, kisses, and caresses. (81)

But she, doubtlessly more realistic, responded to him:

> On your life, the garden did not delight in our union,
> but showed us rancor and envy instead.
> The river did not applaud happy to have us close
> and the turtledove was singing its sorrows.
> Do not think good things the way you usually do,
> for they do not behave well everywhere.
> I do not think the sky showed its stars
> just to spy on us. (81)

In another of her poems, nevertheless, Hafsa expresses her passion, singing the mouth of her beloved:

> I praise those lips because I know

> what I say and I know of what I speak
> and I do them justice, I do not lie before God;
> in them I have drunk a saliva
> more delicious than wine. (82)

There are not lacking, among Hafsa's production, poems with the character of a message.

In this one the theme of the present absent one appears, so characteristic of a love poem:

> I send my greeting,
> that opens the flowers' chalices,
> and makes the dove on the branches speak,
> to a distant friend who lives in my innards
> although my eyes are deprived from seeing him.
> Do not think that absence makes me forget you,
> that, by God, will never happen. (82)

As is natural, the topics and characters representative of the Arabic culture come up also in the work of these women poets. So it is that in one of them, Hafsa identifies Abu Yafar with Yamil, an Udri poet, model of the perfect lover, and herself with her beloved Butayna:

> Am I going to see you or are you coming to my house?
> My heart always bends to your desires.
> You will find yourself safe from the thirst
> and the ardor of the sun
> when you give me the welcome:
> my lips are watery, sweet and fresh,
> and the branches of my tresses give dense shade.
> Answer me quickly: it is not a favor, oh my Yamil
> to make your Butayna wait. (82)

If the writing of poetry was habitual among Arab women, because of their education and profession, even more natural then is the case of the two daughters of a literature professor from the University of Granada, Hamda bint Ziyad and her sister Zaynab. There exists some confusion as to the time in which they lived, but be that as it might, all of the scholars attribute to Hamda the beautiful poem where she describes the young woman who accompanied her on a walk along the banks of a river with a seductive atmosphere, that could be the Genil of Granada or the Arenal of Guadix. Also in this poem the freedom of the woman writer is absolute, and she describes her woman companion just as a male lover would do:

> The tears reveal my secrets
> next to this river where beauty leaves evident traces:
> streams that surround the gardens
> gardens that border the creeks,
> and there is among the gazelles an amicable antelope
> that captivates my mind and possesses my soul,
> he has languid eyes that he closes
> to give orders that prevent me from sleep,
> and when he loosens the hair over his face
> it is the same as the moon
> in the fog of the night,
> and one could say that a friend
> of dawn has died and in sadness
> has dressed itself in mourning. (83)

Persistence Of The Aroma

It is, without a doubt, this great resourcefulness, as much in the relationship with the world as in the use of language, which makes neither the tone nor the images of these poems sound antiquated, but rather, on the other hand, result very current. If we trace coincidences among the Spanish women poets of today and these verses, we shall see that they certainly exist, while the same is not true involving women from the *Cancioneros* or Baroque women –with the exception being María de Zayas-. In the work of a Luisa Sigea, or of a Sister Marcela San Félix (daughter of Lope de Vega and the comic Micaela de Luján), of a Hipólita de Narvaez, of a Cristobalina Fernández de Alarcón or of a Leonor de la Cueva y Silva[6], that has nothing to envy of the writings by men of the period, it is unthinkable to find a tone that approximates not even remotely that of the Arab–Andalusians, so much earlier than they. The Baroque women poets write magnificent commemorative sonnets, full of images and mythological allusions, but they are, above all, very literary.

The present acceptance of this poetry has been prepared by the discovery of the Arabic-Andalusian lyric in general, present in the Hispanic panorama over several decades. The works of Asín Palacios, *The Muslim Scatology of the Divine Comedy* already mentioned, and *The Christianized Islam*, and the studies of Emilio García Gómez who, in addition, converted into Spanish, among other writings, *The Dove's Necklace* by Ibn Hazm, the Arabic-Andalusian

6 See C. Janés, The First Women Poets in the Castilian Language, Endymion, Madrid, 1986.

poems, *Todo Ben Guzman*, and the epigraphic poetry from the Alhambra, opened the terrain and moved the fields of minds as important as those of the Generation of 1927. It is known that Rafael Alberti recognized in his writings the influence of the Arab-Andalusian woman and that García Lorca, who did not do so, had planned his *Tamarit Diván*, nevertheless, with the same García Gómez –after a dinner in a mountain pass, as the latter affirms. To mention another example, almost unknown, and moved by the enthusiasm that the work *The Self-taught Philosopher* by Abentofail inspired in her, the novelist Rosa Chacel conceived an entire novel with the same theme but actualizing it, to which she gave the title of *The Shepherd* and for which she only succeeded in writing one chapter, collected in the work *Novels Ahead of Time*.

That subterranean current, submerged for centuries, has crossed historic periods and their successions and inspired our lyric, whatever its appearance, facet or correspondence might be, that meanwhile has been able to capture, in the same way as avatars, be whatever they may be, the orange tree aromas or "alhelí" flowers that continue flowering each spring. Thus the beauty of fugacity and change is also imposed, which does not escape the woman poet from Guadalajara, Umm al-Ala Bint Yusuf al-Hiyarriya:

> In my garden when the reeds vibrate
> covered in dew,
> it seems that the hand of the winds
> bends some banners over others. (84)

Bibliography

Asín Palacios, M., ed. *La escatología musulmana de la Divina Comedia (Islamic Eschatology of the Divine Comedy)*, Hiperión, Madrid, 1984.

___________. *El Islam cristianizado* (*Christianized Islam*), Hiperión, Madrid, 1981.

García Gómez, E., "Introducción" a Ibn Hazm ("Introduction" to Ibn Hazm), *El collar de la Paloma* (*The Ring of the Dove*), Sociedad de Estudios y Publicaciones, Madrid, 1952.

Garulo, T. *Diván de las Poetisas de Al–Andalus (Divan of Women Poets from Al Andalus)*, Hiperión, Madrid, 1986.

Pérès, H., *Esplendor de Al Andalus (Splendor of Al Andalus)*, Hiperión, Madrid, 1983.

Schack, A. F. von, *Poesía y arte de los árabes en España y Sicilia (Poetry and Art of the Arabs in Spain and Sicily)*, Hiperión, Madrid, 1988.

Sobh, M., *Poetisas arábigo–andaluzas* (*Arabic–Andalusian Women Poets*), Diputación Provincial de Granada, 1986.

V- Love From Afar And Body To Body

Women Troubadours, Warriors and Enlightened Ones

> "Upon arriving at the fort and hearing the news that Hojir had been captured, women and men let out a lament for the loss of the warrior and for their own people who, without him, had become orphans. The daughter of Gadjaham, a valiant amazon woman, having found out that the commander of the fort was missing, decided to go into action. This young woman was famous for her warrior deeds. Her name was Gordafarid and never throughout history had a woman given birth to such a creature. Ashamed because of what had happened to Hojir, her face lit up the color of a tulip, darkened like a fish. There was no time to lose. She put on the warriors' armor and hiding her hair underneath, arranged a Roman helmet on her head. Immediately after she began the descent from the fort, her decision firm and mounting on a fleet horse". (87)

This passage surprises the reader of the *Book of Kings*, of the Persian Firdusi (10th and 11th Centuries), for until it happens, the numerous battle episodes and the beautiful feats did not allow one to suspect a female warrior. Nor does the protagonist of the story, Sohrab, suspect it, and he begins to fight against the one who has shot a rain of arrows upon him, and she defends herself heroically, breaking the lance and fleeing rapidly. But the hero pursues his enemy "bellowing" and then the latter –the narrator tells us– "knowing that she was not capable of competing with him [...] took off her helmet, letting her hair loose and, emerging from the armor, her face "shone like the sun" (87-88). Naturally, Sohrab is astonished and she manages to escape. And not only that, she induces him to follow her to the fort making him believe she will surrender but, upon arriving, she shuts the door on him, climbs to the top of the tower and looks down on him at her feet, disconcerted. She lets out a burst of laughter and says to him: "Why have you bothered? Go back, forget this persecution and abandon the battlefield". And after declaring to him that she is not for him, she concludes: "Don't trust your strong arms too much, the foolish cow prepares herself for death upon satiating her hunger due to the insatiable desire of her body" (88).

The hair of Gordafarid, as one can see, can often appear to be a subtle weapon. It provokes surprise and a moment of pause in the actions, and thus, with this achieved, it becomes a liberator.

Hair will not always have the same character. That of Mélisande, character situated in the Middle Ages and protagonist of Debussy's well known opera, encloses another kind of symbolism. Married to Golaud, Mélisande secretly loves Pelléas, brother of the former, and her love is returned. In a given moment, the lady is combing herself behind the window, when her brother-in-law, from down below, requests that she show herself. She does, and her lengthy locks reach him, and he ties them to a tree so that she cannot leave. A few scenes later, Golaud, jealous, grabs his wife by the hair and abuses her. And even though nothing has happened between her and his brother, they both perish by his sword.

In the case of *Pelléas and Mélisande*, then, hair serves to express the heroine's relationship with both brothers, and in addition, is revealed as a form of punishment, on one hand, and as an amorous connection on the other, which then becomes a part of tradition as hair represents a sum of feminine beauty, and therefore, an element that also incites. As a consequence, to wear it gathered up supposes maturity and caution, and to wear it loose indicates that the step from infancy to adulthood has not yet been taken. The symbol of the beautiful theme of the "girl with hair" is enough of an example (that harkens back to extreme youth and maidenhood) from the traditional Spanish lyric. To sacrifice the mane of hair, on the other hand, represents to renounce the world, a form of death that is demanded, for example, of the woman who enters a convent. Thus, its mere mention can cause us to oscillate between "eros" and "thanatos". This is, without a doubt, the background of the following carol that reaches us as a complaint:

> Now that I am a girl,
> a girl with hair
> you will want to enclose me as a nun
> in the monastery. (89)

The Shadow Of Plato

The thread from the hair –weapon, amorous seduction, and resignation– leads us toward three feminine faces, three types of women fundamental in the Middle Ages – a period of contrasts–: the female troubadour, the woman religious and the warrior. And also for them the possibilities can be developed in angles.

Ortega y Gasset, in his prologue to the work of Ibn Hazm, *The Dove's Necklace*, places us before some evidence that until now had barely been suspected: the importance of the contact from a large part of Europe –not just the countries from the South, such as Spain– with the Arab world. He considers it, then, an error to look toward the continent just from a western perspective. Ortega y Gasset points out "the cohabitation, positive and negative at the same time, of Christianity and Islam *throughout a common area impregnated by the Greco-Roman culture*. The Islamic religion itself stems from the Christian one –it is said– but this origin could not have taken place, at the same time, if the European and Arab peoples had not penetrated in the area occupied for centuries by the Roman Empire. Germanics and Arabs were marginal peoples, lodged on the borders of that Empire". (89)

Following on these important words, the philosopher analyzes the reception of the Classical culture by those primitive cultures, and also the genesis of the Christian culture in relation to the Arabic one. The Islamic peoples –he observes–, already in the 9th Century had been introduced to the work of Aristotle, Hippocrates, Galen, Euclid, Diophantus or Ptolemy, and had been relatively hellenized for at least seven centuries, due to the fact that, not only Syria but also Persia, Bactria, and even India, had lived under the administration of the Roman Empire, which did not happen in Northern Europe. He says concretely: "The only initial difference –which is, without a doubt, important–, stems from the fact that the Arabs received Antiquity in its form from the Eastern Roman Empire, and the Europeans in its form from the Western Roman Empire" (90). And he adds that, in both cases, Islam and Germanic Christianity, there was a point of origin in the Church fathers.

This point of origin is important because it orients the way of looking at life, it implicitly carries an appreciation of seclusion, a concentration of the "I" on a move toward the inner self, from which, forcefully, one has to emerge with great intensity. Such intensity is the same as that which surrounds the fundamental concept of love, which concerns the three types of women cited here: troubadours, religious and warriors. Regarding the first, it is made specific through the exaltation of the values of the female in the courts of Provence; in the religious area, in monasticism, and in particular, in the case of isolation that allows for studying and unveiling of divine science, and on the battlefield, the aforementioned intensity can provoke, on some occasion by illumination, the perseverance of the young woman who, with a shield and helmet, prepares herself for battle, even though she might end up in the bonfire, like Joan of Arc.

The importance of Platonism is not foreign to these ideas

–it was recovered in Alexandria and by the Islamic thinkers–, and it defines the world as a shadow and love, equally, as a reminiscence of something seen once, and that brings with it virtues so strong as to cause the genesis of life. Certainly Platonism seems to infiltrate in the vital horizons of the moment, in concrete cases because, in order to tolerate the real, one takes refuge in the ideal, or because the Augustine norm of *per visibilia ad invisibilia* was followed, that oriented the first anchorites toward the Egyptian dessert, in whose ways the Sufis were inspired, as affirms Asín Palacios.

Plato's doctrine played an important part among the Arabs and, in first place, the already mentioned Udri love, also called the love of Baghdad, practiced by the tribe of the "banu 'udra" (the sons of virginity), those who died upon being denied the delight of the loved one. García Gómez highlights among his prototypes Urwa, Kutayu, Chamil y Machnún (the Crazy One), who, separated from Layla by her marriage to someone else, retired to the desert and lived in solitude dedicated to poetry and to exalting physical renunciation, because the beloved –he would affirm– was found within him. Machnún, then, would sing a "remote" love that only reached its true fulfillment in death. *Eros* and *Thanatos*, yes, presence in absence, quest for an impossible absolute, vocation of death. All of this entailed, without a doubt, a seed of Romanticism.

The connection between the Udris and the troubadours is an accepted fact. In the "love courts" of Provence, in fact, man considered woman as superior, he worshipped her, as a vassal, and he placed her off *in the distance,* "in remote camber, like the star" (Ortega). From this the troubadour, who would sing to her, cultivated the lament, even if in this case it did not have to do with a complete renunciation, but with a desire for everything, but from "de lonh", from a distance.

The expression "love from a distance" was coined by the troubadour Jaufre Rudel (12th Century), whom the Romantics hoisted decidedly as a hero. In love from a distance with the Countess of Tripoli, the bard not only sang of her but left for the Crusades in order to see her. He had fallen seriously ill, that news was carried to the Countess, and she came immediately to his bedside. Jaufre died in her arms praising God, who had permitted him to see her; and the Countess, moved by the sorrow, entered into a convent.

Denis de Rougement, in *Love and the Western World* (and pointing also to the Cathars), observes: "a great Manichean religious current, which had its source in Iran, goes back to Asia Minor and the Balkans up to Italy and France, bringing its esoteric doctrine of the Sophia-Maria and of love in the 'form of light. ' On the other hand, a highly refined rhetoric, with its procedures, its themes and constant characters, its ambiguities, that are always reborn in the same places, and finally its symbolism, goes back to Iraq and the Platonic and Manichean Sufis and up to Arab Spain, and, passing over the Pyrenees, finds in Midi a society that, apparently, did not expect more than those means of language to say what could not be dared or confessed in the language of the clerics or in the vulgar tongue. *Courtly poetry was born of this encounter*". Some lines before he has written: "The precise prose of the zéjel is the same as reproduced by the first troubadour, William of Poitiers, in five of the 11 poems that are left to us" (91-92).

Nobody today doubts, in fact, the real contact of those two worlds: The Arabs arrived, precisely, up to Poitiers, where they were defeated by Charles Martel in the year 732. (A comparative study of the use of these words by the troubadours and the Arabic and Persian poets would throw still more light on the question). On the other hand, there are examples with concrete quotations, such as the hymn of Saint Martial of Limoges, written in language of L'Occitane in the 11th Century, which says:

> My friends and my faithful
> leave the ghazal be
> learn a new melody
> of the Virgin Mary. (92)

To Sing What One Might Not Want

A kind of connection between the mystical and the warrior (*eros* and *thanatos*, I insist), a buckle –to continue with the hair metaphor– is produced from the attitude having to do with love in the court of Provence. This is made concrete, on one hand, by that direct contact with the ideas of a platonizing nature, that besides, Denis de Rougement, in his exalting of chastity, connects to a movement extensive in India since the 6th Century connected to the "initially cosmic feminine" cult; and, on the other hand, in the way of making hers the warrior terminology. He says concretely: "The lover besieges the beloved. He throws himself into amorous assaults on her virtue. He *stalks* her, he *pursues* her, he intends *to conquer* the last *defenses* of her modesty, and *to take her by surprise*; finally the *woman surrenders unconditionally*. But then, by a curious inversion very typical of courtesy, it is the lover who will be her *prisoner* at the same time as her *conqueror*. He will become a vassal of that lady according to the law of the feudal wars, exactly as if he were the one who had undergone the "defeat". These are, then, the important points: irradiant love and the sword of death. And thus, the heroic troubadour spirit moves between the glare of the unattainable love and the mortal tear of desire.

Now then, when the woman expresses herself, the defeat becomes another and brings us closer to de Rougement's observation about courtly love that, he affirms, does not deal with, as has been said, an opting for mysticism as preached by Saint Bernard, but rather, on the contrary, is "the poetic expression of concupiscence". Thus are produced verses as direct as those of the Countess of Dia, who in her time was compared with Sappho of Lesbos:

> Beautiful friend, kind and good;
> when will I have you in my power?
> and be able to lie with you one night
> and give you a kiss of love!
> Know that, as much as I would like
> to have you in the place of the husband,
> as long as you had sworn to
> to do everything I would like. (93)

After centuries of struggle, customs had become more refined, and with the birth of chivalry –whose spirit, observed Hegel, was also of Eastern origin, even though the barbarism had not disappeared completely, woman began to occupy a place in society.

In the troubadour courts, the women, who are its "queens", support literature, which, in a certain way, anticipates those who, later, in the 17th Century, will open salons, whose influence will be decisive in developing language. The fame of the noble protector women begins to extend itself. Thus it is that the names of Ermengarde of Narbonne, Eleanor of Toulouse, Azalais of Marseille, Gursenda, Beatrice of Provence, Beatrice of Montferrat, Maria of Ventadorn, Juana and Constance of Esse or the countess Beatritz of Dia. "Parties of love" are organized, and they revolve around the married woman, and that "courtly love" of "fin'amors", is practiced, according to which the "divinized woman", except on rare occasions, is inaccessible, and the troubadour becomes her vassal and unconditional servant.

But as we saw, not only the troubadour sings to the woman, but she also sings. Since the year 1160 one hears of poets in the South of France, while in the North Maria of France stands out. This author, identified at times with Marie of Champagne, daughter of Leonor of Aquitaine, at the end of the 12th century writes the *Lais*, brief narrative poems that celebrate love and are a milestone in their moment and precursors –together with the novels of Chrétien of Troyes– from the Arthurian literature. In the other cultured towns, with the exception of the Arab ones, poetry in the Middle Ages is the dominion of men.

The female Provençal poets, in general, or they belong to the highest society, like the countess of Dia, the Countess of Provence or the Vice–countess of Ventadorn, or are either of noble ascendance, like Isabel or Almuc of Castellnou. According to the cases, they are called "gentle lady" (*gentil donna*), or simply *na* or *donna*, and also *midons*, from the Latin *mi señor* ("My Lord"), because when the husbands left for the Crusades, according to the researchers, the women would take charge not only of the coffers but also of the reins.

The complete identification of these women poets is almost impossible, but some minimal data usually appear in the "Life" statement that accompanies the poems. Thus in that of the Countess Beatritz of Dia, we read: "She was the wife of William of Poitiers, beautiful woman and good; and she fell in love with Rimbaut d'Aurenga, and wrote for him good and beautiful verses". These lines are a manifestation of a passionate temperament. Four of her songs and *a tensó* –that is, a dialogue, a dispute– between her and Rimbaut d'Aurenga. For the society then, Beatritz of Dia's daring was unheard of:

> Merit and nobility should serve me for something,
> beauty and, even more, faithful heart.
> For that reason I send to your dwelling,
> a messenger of mine, with this song.
> I want to know, gentle and beautiful friend,
> why you are so distant and so cruel with me,
> I do not know if it is due to ill will or to haughtiness.
> (95)

This strophe is almost the conclusion of her most celebrated poem, at times compared with Ovid's *Heroides*, in part because of the use of the verse form of greater length. I refer to the one that begins as follows:

> I want to sing what I would not like,
> such uneasiness my friend provokes in me,
> for more than anything in the world I love him.
> With him neither pity nor courtesy serves me,
> nor beauty, nor merit nor judgment,
> now that I am deceived and betrayed,
> in the same way as if I were absent. (95)

The poems of the Countess of Dia belong to the school of *trovar leu* ("light poetry"), being one of the best representatives of this style due to the simplicity of its writing. It does not use, in general, complicated rhymes, but in one of the songs, the only one that appears joyous and optimistic, makes use of the "derivative" rhyme, that associates the masculine and feminine with an adjective, the simple and compound, and the diverse forms of a simple verb[7], which carries with it a singular musicality:

> Ab joi et ab joven m'apais
> et jois et jovens m'apaia
> car mos amics es lo plus gais
> per qu'ieu sui coindet'e gaia;
> e pois eu li sui verais,
> c'anc de lui amar no m'estrais
> ni ai cor que me'n estraia. (95–96)

> [I nourish myself with joy and youth,
> and joy and youth nourish me,

7 This type of games are very frecuent in Persian poetry, for example.

and, since my friend is the most joyous,
I am happy and graceful;
and as I will be true,
it is only just that he be the same,
since I never strayed from loving him
nor do I have intention of straying from him.] (96)

To Take A Husband Or Remain A Maiden

Beatritz of Dia also makes use of some formulae that had some tradition within the Provençal lyric, as in the verses, "at times one reaches for the whip / with which to lash oneself". (Janés, Spanish translation, 96). In one of the songs she utilizes the twist, in order to say "always: " "in bed and when I am dressed", more daring than other common expressions, like "winter and summer", "night and day", "morning and afternoon", to help make the same idea understood.

The number of songs composed by women troubadours that have reached us is 46. At times the "Life" statement says little about them and, on the other hand, they are often quoted in "Life and Reasonings" (texts that give some notice of the bard's poems), such as Alamanda de Castelnau, who appears in the *reasonings* of her interlocutor, Giraut de Bornelh, or Clara d'Anduza, who figures in a *reasoning* of Uc de Saint Circ. In both cases, this has to do with a *tensó* (dispute). In the first, Giraut asks Alamanda to intercede on his behalf with his wife and she reproaches the mistakes made by him regarding his wife, although she ends up promising him help, but warns him:

"By God, Giraut, for once / the desires of a friend are not realized" (97).

As far as Uc de Saint Circ there is simply a relationship with Clara d'Anduc mentioned. She, for her part, expresses that desire as love and, on not seeing it fulfilled, as suffering:

> May the sweet longing that I have for you not increase,
> nor the anxiety, nor the desire, nor the temptation.
> [....]
> Friend, such sorrow and discomfort I feel
> upon not seeing you now, that when I plan to sing
> I cry and sigh, because I can't do it. (97)

The songs of women troubadours are limited to love songs. Gormonda, in verses, remembers nothing less than the figure of Merlin:

> But that which Merlin
> said in a prophecy,
> of the good King Louis,
> who will die in Montpellier. (97)

This reference in a prophecy about the death of King Louis XI of France is the only one within the troubadour poetry that traces back to the Arthurian cycle. Another interesting reference is the one that Azalais of Porcairagues makes, in this case to Ovid:

> As Ovid has pronounced
> love does not select wealth. (97)

The "Life" of Azalais says that "she was from the region of Montpellier, gentle lady and cultured. And she fell in love with Giraut Geurejat, the brother of Gilhem of Montpellier. And the lady was accustomed to singing and she created some very good songs for him" (97). In the poem fragment that has reached us, she speaks of her amorous relationships and of how they are advancing and how one must keep on without giving in to temptation. She begins, in any case, by framing the poem in a landscape.

> Now that we have arrived at the cold weather,
> with snow, ice and mud,
> and the little bird finds itself mute,
> and not inclined to sing;
> and in the hedges, the branches are dry,
> neither leaves nor flowers grows in them,
> nor does the nightingale sing,
> that later in May reveals itself to me.
> [............]
> I have a friend of great value
> who reigns above everyone,
> and does not have a traitorous heart,
> since he surrenders his love to me.
> I say that my love I award it,
> and may God bring bad luck;
> to he who says I do not,
> for I consider myself safe.
>
> Beautiful friend, of good humor
> without ceasing under your domain
> are courtesy and your beautiful face,
> as long as you do not demand an insult;
> soon we will do the test;
> since I will surrender myself to your lord;
> you have sworn me to faith
> do not ask me to commit a mistake! (98)

And she concludes remembering her patrons, Ermengarde of Narbonne:

> Minstrel of a joyous heart,
> carry my song with the message
> to Narbonne, which is guided by
> youth and joy. (98)

It can happen, as in the case of Beatriz of Romans, that a woman could be the addressee of the poem. Rene Nelli, in the first volume of *Anticonformist Writers of the Western Middle Ages,* offers this text of hers: *Na Maria, pretz e fina valors ("Lady Maria, for her beauty, nobility, and many other virtues").*

> Lady Maria, subtle value and merit,
> joy, sprit and rare beauty,
> your way of welcoming and honoring your value,
> your amicable language and suave conversation,
> your gentile face and exquisite ways,
> your gaze and amorous aspect,
> all of these unparalleled qualities
> have attracted my heart without any villainy. (99)

And completing the specter of the feminine Provençal soul, is the dispute (*"tensó"*) that dates from around 1280) between Alais, Iselda and Carenza, in which the first of these ask for advice regarding their situation:

> — Lady Carenza, of beautiful and affable body,
> welcome the two sisters that we are
> since you know how to select the best,
> advise us according to your judgment,
> Should I, according to you, take a husband
> or remain a maiden? This selection pleases me more,

for having children does not tempt me,
but it is bitter to remain without a husband. (99)

— Doña Alais and Doña Iselda,
good education, merit, beauty, good color,
you have all of this, and courtesy,
and intensity more than others and the best.
I advise you, for your own good,
to take a husband crowned by knowledge.
With him you will engender a splendid child.
Precious is a virgin for the one who marries her. (99)

Shouts And Laughter

The possibilities of selection by the female were not exactly numerous. Besides matrimony, the other graceful way out was the convent. But in those times of conflict there arose, suddenly, another figure who was revealed as a daring adventurer, I refer to the "religious women", that is, those who were still living religion deeply but did not submit themselves to the norms of a monastery. Among them, the so-called "Beguines", who, without having taken vows and distancing themselves from institutions, lived during the century, and also the "recluses" or "walled in" women, whose life was analogous to that of the hermits and anchorites but transferred to the city, where they dwelled in cells built up against the walls of churches. These portrayed their inner experience, at times at risk of life, such as Margarita Porete who died burned by the Inquisition. These women, like the troubadours, recognized a love from a distance –they even used the same expression, *amor de lonh*–; an inaccessible love, whose reach, in this case more through vision, even though also by the word, would culminate in paradox: that which was far, was in the same interior depths of the soul.

Protected by the belief of finding themselves before a divine revelation, these "religious women" are even less contained than the "ladies" ("damas") in their expressions, and they laugh boisterously, cry and shout. We seem to hear still the incomprehensible voice of Angela of Foligno, who upon arriving at the gate of the Basilica of Assisi and seeing the stained glass attributed to Cimabue where San Francisco is represented hugging Jesus, erupts in exclamations with these words: "Unknown love, why are you leaving me? Unknown love, why and why and why?" She experienced visions that pushed her to penetrate in the wound of Christ and to drink his blood, despite the fact that she would finish her days with the powerful cry: "Oh unknown nothingness? Oh unknown nothingness!" (100).

The step that these women take toward a depth of wisdom is enormous, and they take it because they face the absolute distance of the unknown with all of their being, that is, also through the senses, –which they do not hide–, and, besides, many of them, thanks to their detachment, even receive their food through a little window. That is, like the Brahman Hindus, who could not have food in their houses because their goal was to be completely devoted to thought, which resulted in the unsurpassed writing of the Upanishad, nor can these women devote themselves to anything else that is not that devotion to vision and meditation. Thus, the irrevocable force of memory, of everything they have seen and done since their birth, which has captured their sensibility and which their hidden depths have stored, is within reach and makes this question of "why" be necessarily connected to the religious experience, an experience of love in the end, of that God in whom is fused the complexity of being one and three, creator and thus father and mother, of being and not being, absent present, love, yes, "de lonh" (from a distance), manifested through visions. These visions, even though directly connected to the Bible and other books and knowledge that they have been able to store up, require interpretation.

The laughter in which Juliana of Norwich breaks out (from the 14th Century), the most audacious in these concepts, when she says as regards sin: "I saw that our Lord belittled his evil and scorned it as if it were nothing. And he wants us to do the same" –which caused her to write that famous sentence pointed out centuries later by Aldous Huxley and T. S. Eliot: "Sin is necessary, but everything will turn out in the end. And everything will turn out well, and each thing, no matter what it may be, will turn out well"– and this supposes such a daring so great as that of her compatriot and contemporary Margery Kempe. The latter, after giving birth to 14 children, at the age of 40, abandons her family to freely undertake a life of mercy, in an errant way, and to make pilgrimages to the Holy Land, Assisi, Rome, Santiago and (even over 60) to Aachen, suffering the accusation of Lollardism[8] and, as a consequence, various trials, and to later dictate her autobiography where she does not hide her tears and her cries born from religious emotion.

8 Lollardism, also known as **Lollardy** or the Lollard movement, was a Proto-Protestant Christian religious movement that existed from the mid-14th century until the 16th-century English Reformation.

The books of these women, that gathered visions and messages directly "revealed", often became, in effect and with frequency, daring, a kind of daring that was emphasized in many cases by the use of common language. If the exegesis of the *Song of Songs*, from which originated the notion of mystic love, could seem discrete in Latin, carried out in the spoken language and besides, with those touches of *amor de lonh* or "at a distance", it seemed alarming. As much then as now, that love that was in principle inaccessible, could become transformed, in the words of Hadewijch, into the "fury of love". And thus already in the Council of Lyon, as regards the "women religious", one spoke of scandal.

Given everything, since the 13th Century, these mystics were considered masters due to their experience and the charisma of the revealed word. Now then, a woman inspired by grace could be a doctor in theology *ex beneficio* but not *ex oficio* and, in no case could she exercise "directing herself to men but rather *in silence, privately, not in public nor in front of the church*", as Victoria Cirlot and Blanca Garí affirm in their book *The Interior Gaze: Mystic Writers and Visionaries in the Middle Ages*. In spite of all that, her voice would emerge in an uncontainable way, such as that of Hildegarde de Bingen, because God "ordered her to write", or that of Margarita de Oingt because "she wrote or she died". Be that as it was, their importance in the spiritual field became notorious, since (as the aforementioned authors say), "they represented the live testimony of the existence of God [and…] to such an extent that correspondences between the feminine and the experience of God were established, and that in the 14th Century mystic males had to become feminized" (102).

Hildegard of Bingen (11th Century) –whose gifts included, besides writing, music and prophecy–, a visionary since the age of three, lived in a cell from the time she was 14 and only at 24 did she leave in order to preach and to become the Abbess of Rubertsberg. In her first prophetic work titled *Scivias* ("Know the ways"), she gathers together 26 visions, among them the following one:

> I saw a kind of great mountain that was the color of iron. And above this mountain was seated a being of great clarity who caused my face to reverberate. From each of the sides a shadow spread out, like a wing of admirable length and width. And in front of him at the foot of the mountain was an image full of eyes, for which, with the exception of the eyes, I was not capable of discerning a human form. And in front of this was another figure of infantile age dressed in a yellow tunic but with white footwear, and above the head such clarity descended that I could not make out the face. From the one seated on the mountain sprang a multitude of live sparks that flew around those images with a great sweetness. (102)

The Soul Or The Imagination

Two other visions inspire Hildegard to first write *Book of the Merits of Life*, and later on, *Book of the Divine Works*, both equally prophetic, the last one motivated by a vision she had in 1163, whose event she relates in this way: "Sometime after, I saw a marvelous and mysterious vision, in such a way that all of my innards were shaken and the sensuality of my body extinguished. My knowledge changed in such a way that I almost did not know myself. Drops of soft rain from God's inspiration spread throughout the conscience of my soul, like the Holy Spirit that drenched St. John the Evangelist when he sucked the profound revelation from the breast of Christ, through which his senses were touched by the holy divinity and hidden mysteries and works revealed to him, upon saying 'At the beginning there was the verb' " (103).

Hildegard, in order to relate this experience, expresses herself following the Cistercian spirituality, and concretely a treatise from the 12th Century, the *Speculum virginum* where, among other Biblical texts, is included *The Song of Songs*. Undoubtedly the accessibility of the *Song of Songs* read in the divine way characterized the visionary expressions. But it is worthy of pointing out that several of the symbolisms employed by the Abbess of Rupertsberg are found in Islamic Mysticism including before Ibn Arabi, contemporary of the nun and called, by the way, "son of Plato", for whom the angels had been created from light and the imagination coming from the corporealization of things, and for that reason affirmed that the soul was made of imagination.

Previous to him, Al-Hallach (10th Century), made use of numerous mystic symbols. One could say that in his poems he moved past everything that constituted the specter of said literature. One of them begins this way:

> Silence, then mutism, then muteness / and knowledge,
> then discovery, and then dust on the tomb,
> mud, then fire, then light / and cold, then shadow
> then sun,

> and rock, then plain, then desert, / and river, then sea, then mainland,
> and drunkenness, then lucidity, then desire, / and next, then surrender, then pleasure,
> and contraction, then extension, then suppression, / and
> separation, then reunion, then erasure (103-104)

Regarding the binomial light-shadow, Hildegard affirms: "my soul does not lack at any moment the light that I call shadow of the living light". These words are similar to the metaphoric games of Ibn Arabi, for example, when he says: "He knows that that which is designated as other than God, has the same relationship with God as the shadow with the person (who projects it) [...]. The world is only known to the extent in which the shadows are known". And although Hildegard does not reach the extremes that the Beguines do, for whom the annihilated soul is transformed into "that which is God" –point of identification analogous to that formulated by Al Hallach, who affirmed: "I am the Truth", that is, "I am God", which caused him to be crucified and dismembered– for her, the soul, "in the peak of the vision becomes the same as God" (104).

Hildegard writes these prophetic visions in a highly apocalyptical tone. She had other gifts in addition –apart from that of writing and that of music, already mentioned– that is, she enjoyed certain charismas. Her works, some of which have reached us beautifully illuminated, are also an indication of the importance that she had in that moment.

As we can see, no matter the pathway, the connections

with Eastern Mysticism are evident. Certainly "the crazy people of God" were connected to Islam, and they called themselves Sufis, in imitation of Machnún, that emblematic person from the Banu Udrah tribe. And I affirm here that another of these "religious women", Beatrice of Nazareth, learned the copyist trade, submitted herself to rigorous fasting, and later thought about appearing crazy, precisely in the way of the "crazies of God" who dwelled in the desert, in order to be closer to Christ for suffering more insults. She also reacted when confronted by her visions with uncontrolled crying and laughter.

On the other hand, the already mentioned Margarita Porete was a Beguine, it appears, from those called *girόvagas* (another term used by the Sufis), that is, for those who wandered the roads. Because of their work, *Mirror of the Simple Souls* was burned in Paris by the Inquisition.

Porete, basing herself on the language of the courtiers, gave God the name of *Loing-pres* (because "the far off is really close, because the soul knows in itself the distance as actually near. [...] and all is for her a oneness without a why, and she is nothing in that oneness". This is the point of the mystic annihilation ("suppression; " "erasure"). Porete affirmed: "The soul receives its true name from the nothingness where it resides and since she is nothing, nothing is important to her, not herself, not her fellow man, not God himself/herself", a daringness that even surpasses Hallach's, and, like with him, provided martyrdom to her (105).

Another daring vision was that of Margarita de Oingt,

who contemplated the body of a Christ Mother giving birth, in the moment of her death. She employed the symbolism of three colors, as much on speaking the letters as speaking of the Trinity, and she saw herself as a dry tree, which the water of life would turn green (another Islam topic, that already appears in Ansari, born at the beginning of the11th Century).

Inferno Of Love

But literarily perhaps the most interesting case might be that of Matilde of Magdeburg, that, in a German sprouting outside the norms, adjusted to express the inexpressible, and that Enrique de Nordlingen considered the most "marvelous and strangest", wrote the book revelation *The Flowing Light of Divinity*, where, fusing with the cosmological-symbolic sphere is one parallel to the courtly *minnesang* ("love song"). Her thought also ended up in nothingness.

Matilde of Magdeburg wrote, in effect, in a state of mystical inspiration and combined poetry and prose. Born in 1207, at 23 she abandoned the family home, settled in Magdeburg and became a Beguine. Then she moved to the monastery of Hefte. The edition of the aforementioned book, *The Flowing Light*, took her 15 years. She explained it in this way: "I don't want to and I can't write if I don't see it with the eyes of my soul and if I don't hear it with the ears of my eternal spirit and if I don't feel in all the members of my body the force of the Holy Spirit" (106-

106). And since she did not know Latin, she wrote in German and always with a view toward the informulable, and also with a background from the *Song of Songs*. Thus says one of her poems:

> Then Our Lord spoke:
> Stop yourself, Soul!
> What do you want, My Lord?
> You have to become nude!
> Lord, how will that happen?
> You are so at home in my being
> that nothing can get between you and me.
> To no angel was it conceded
> what has been given to you until Eternity.
> For that reason you need to leave to one side
> fear and shame
> and all of the external virtues.
> Only those that naturally live in you
> you should care for them eternally:
> This is your noble longing and desire without end
> that I want to fill eternally with my infinite generosity.
> Lord, and you in yourself a god richly adorned.
> Our community
> is eternal life without death.
> Then there took place a beatific silence
> according to both desires.
> He surrendered himself to her and she to him.
> That which happened to the soul, she knows it
> and that gives me much consolation.
> But it did not last long.
> For when two lovers find each other secretly
> they often have to separate without farewell. (106)

The daringness of her writing, so close to the amorous profane, was, probably, that which caused her text to be translated to Latin, thus initiating a custom that would be repeated with the work of Margarita Porete.

And not only the style of Matilde of Magdeburgo was daring, but rather its content. She would affirm, for example, that when the soul "elevates itself with great desires toward God [...] the body also earns its part, in such a way that all will be formed through love" (107). To this emphasis in love is united a radicalism comparable to that of the master Eckhart, everything disguised in a negative mystic, for the surrender required descending to the infernos and "drowning oneself in darkness" and abandoning themselves to the desert, the place of absolute absence:

> You should love the nothingness,
> you should flee to the "I",
> you should be alone
> and not get close to anyone [...].
> You should drink the water of sorrow
> and light the embers of love on the wood of virtues;
> in this way you will live in the true desert. (107)

Equally unique is the enlightened Hadewijch of Antwerp, of whom the only thing we know is that she wrote between 1235 and 1244, that she was very cultured, dominated the Dutch language –that she used in her texts–, but also Latin and likely French. It is deduced, based on her knowledge –among them that of the troubadour lyric–, that she was educated in an ambience of nobility and had access to poetic and musical teachings. Her writing reflects the chivalric spirit, the errant search, the quest, the tests, the adventure and all of the courtly code surrounding the Lady of Love. She was a teacher and Beguine, and as such, likely dedicated herself to the service of her fellow man/woman in the city, for example by caring for sick people. Her belief in love as knowledge and the impossibility of satisfying it as the most elevated form of itself, caused her to revindicate not submitting herself to a rule but because in doing so "one surrenders to a thousand concerns from which it would have been better to be free, for thus is reason mistaken" (107.

Her poems take in a wide spectrum in all senses. Some, spontaneous and lively, seem born from the lips of the Sufi Turk Yunus Emre, thus this ending to one of them:

> —Cheers, cheers, a thousand times –friends,
> take the side of God,
> — to say it is not enough—
> in the pardon or in the justice. (108)

These lines belong to one of his stanza poems. Within those of this genre, themes such as the following appear: dissolution of the soul, abyss without end, and the storm or furor of love. Thus in the poem that follows, we are reminded of the troubadours, where it says:

> The furor of love
> is a rich fiefdom;
> he who recognizes that
> will not ask anything more of Love:
> it can unite opposites,
> invert the senses.
> [...]
> It displays everything
> as much as can be learned
> in the high school of Love.

In the high school of Love,
one learns the furor of love. (108)

And throwing herself into the game of oppositions, the mystic of Antwerp ends up anticipating the Baroque thought structures:

So quickly burning, so quickly cold,
now timid and audacious an instant ago,
the caprices of love are numerous [...]
so quickly gentile, so quickly terrible,
nearby now, far off an instant ago [...]
so quickly light, so quickly heavy,
dark now, clear an instant ago. (108)

Three well-defined groups constitute the writings of Hadewijch: *The Strophic Poems and Poems of Mixed Rhyme*, the *Letters* and *Book of Visions*. One of the poems of mixed rhyme deals with the seven names that "reveal all of the essence and ways of beautiful love", and thus calls it: *Link*, *light*, *coal*, *fire*, *dew*, *lively fountain* and *inferno*, this last name summarizing the paradox of love as negation:

He who has known love and its comings and goings
has felt and can understand,
why it is truly appropriate
that Inferno be the highest of the names for Love. (109)

Hadewijch influenced Jan van Ruysbroeck, in whose work arise themes typical of the mystic of Antwerp: a measuring angel, the inverted tree of knowledge, the non-love (or without love) ...

Pure rapture and exercise of risk are the writings of these

enlightened women and, with everything, in spite of the times that were, they found defenders among the Church hierarchies and including some friars and clerics who took note of their words, put themselves at their service and wrote of their lives. In this way their texts have reached us, which continue to surprise us. It becomes comprehensible that their impassioned and disconcerting personalities, with their voices and forms of expression, would provoke scandal for they dared to sing, for example, as did Hadewijch, "the mutual devouring of Christ and the soul in the Eucharist" (109).

Devouring, inferno, love of nothingness and challenge to death; and also to receive and give it, because the cross was equally that of the sword, and to wield an arm could signify the "furor of love" (109).

Sacred Furor

From the cell, isolation, the mastery of "science revealed", the divine amorous clamor, we move to the dust raised by horses, to the sound of armor, to the art of strategy and warrior cry. "Saint Jordi!", "Arago!", which was that of the Almogavars, who fought during the Fourth Crusade and, among them the chronicler Ramón Muntaner, who relates the confrontation of Galípoli, castle located in the narrowest part of the Dardanelos peninsula –during which the fight was led "poorly accompanied by men but well by women", whose fury surprised him–. They were the ones, apparently (and the number 2,000 is often quoted) who managed to reject the attack of the Genoeses commanded by Boccanegra. This took place in the 14th Century. God, justice and truth were their slogans, because, "all of the victories are due to the will of God" (110).

But already since the beginnings of the Crusades, some women would depart wielding a sword (some because of their trade, the prostitutes), and there were those who accompanied their consorts: many queens and ladies of high nobility. With time, the Pope prohibited it through indulgence, precisely at the time the Third Crusade began, but despite all that, it is said that Eleanore of Aquitaine, Berengaria of Navarre, wife of Richard the Lionheart, Florin of Denmark and Margarita of Provenza fought in it while, according to Gilbert de Nogent, the Emperor Conrad II entered into war in Syria with a "troup of horsewomen" (110).

The Crusades was a great adventure and everybody corroborated: gunsmiths, blacksmiths, tailors, tanners, different artisans that supplied food, women who would make clothing and winter garments, they embroidered flags, emblems, pennants, flags … the Pope supported them and the clerics encouraged them from the cathedrals and the pulpits, preaching their purpose and igniting the "sacred furor" (110). Thus, words oriented to rescue the Holy Sepulchre unleashed an irrational fury that led to killings not only of Jews but also of Christians who practiced Easter rituals (Syrians, Coptics, Armenians, Georgians, Greeks), and thus conquest and heroism presented themselves along with robbery and reproach. An ambiguous flame burned that united the instinct of affirmation with inculcated faith, moved by the verbal thunder of the maximum Church authority.

The defense of papal interests precisely reveals an undeniable warrior: Matilda of Tuscany or of Canosa, daughter of Bonifacio III of Tuscany and Beatriz of Lotaringia. Born in 1046, Matilda lost her father at the age of six and her mother, by her own initiative, contracted second nuptials with Godrey the Bearded Man, Duke of Alta Lorena, thus awakening the ire of the Emperor Henry III. Beatrice went out, then, with the intention of giving some explanations (the emperor, of course, took advantage to take her prisoner), leaving the little girl at home. There, under the tutelage of Arduin della Padulle, Matilda learned the use of weapons, chivalry and military art (according to Lodovico Vedriani, some of her military armor was conserved until the 17th Century in the *Four Castles*: Montesano, Montelucio, Montevetro and Bibianello).

According to the legend, if indeed there are no facts that prove it, Matilda participated for the first time in a battle (along with her mother) when she was only 15 years old. It had to do with supporting Alexander II. Some historians affirm that she wanted to renounce the world, but the same Pope obliged her to get married, which she did in 1071 with Godfrey IV the Humpback Man, Duke of Lower Lotaringia, and when he died (1076), she contracted a new marriage, with Guelph IV, Duke of Bavaria.

Matilda of Tuscany was very influential due to her political and military actions. She controlled all of the Italian territories from the North of the States belonging to the

Church that, in 1076, included: Lombardy, Emilia, Romagna and Tuscany (with the center in Canosa). But her power not only resided in her possessions and in her knowledge of bellicose arts, but also in other capacities: she spoke, for example, the Teuton language, that of the "Francs" and she could write in Latin.

With everything, her distinctive trait was on the battlefield; with her stepfather murdered, she set up to avenge him, sword in hand. She was the greatest ally of Gregory VII and participated in mediation between him and Henry IV during the Investiture Controversy. In fact, she spent 30 years in warfare, herself as commander of the troops, until in 1114 she retired to a Benedictine convent, where she died *–strength and wisdom–* as the medieval slogan prayed.

Not always did the female put on a breastplate to defend the Pope or recover the Holy Sepulchre. Some years before Matilda's death, in 1090, the Duchess Gaita of Lombardy also died, and she was, they say, wearing complete armor to fight in battles next to her husband, a Norman mercenary.

In Spain, in those days, Queen Urraca I of León (1081-1126) stood out; daughter of King Ferdinand I of Castille, who, by the law of León that granted her "juridical capacity to exercise royal power in all of its reaches and due right" (Angel G. Gordo Molina, 112). And, upon becoming the widow of the Count Raimundo, she became *regent*, and then empress. Separated from her second husband, Alfonso I of Aragón, and in constant discord with him and her stepsister Teresa of Portugal, in comings and goings of agreements and hostilities, unfulfilled pacts, concessions or changes in alliances... Dressed in armor, she herself recruited men, prepared the army, planned the battles, and would move with her hosts through inhospitable places, resting in pavilions and not castles. We see her on horseback, sheathed in breastplate and helmet, in charge of the siege of Carrión in defense of the rights of her son to the throne, just as she had defended her own when Ferdinand I was on his deathbed, as battle-hardened as the ballad presents her when she hurls this reproach at him:

> You wish to die, father,
> may Saint Michael keep your soul;
> you sent your lands
> to those who pleased you...
> [...]
> And me, because I am a woman
> you leave me disinherited. (112)

The chronicle describes her as indomitable and fearless. In effect, the words she uses to threaten her dying father, when confronted with this treatment, could not be more daring:

> I will go around these lands
> like a woman wronged,
> and this my body I would give up,
> to the Moors for money,
> and to the Christians for grace,
> and conquer what I could
> and do good for your soul. (112)

The official ballad collection does not always include these stories, nor the one of the "Warrior Maiden", transvestite of Don Martín. They had their base and, even though in the Middle Ages the gentleman knight was of *miles christi* (Soldiers of Christ), ("land bounded by men"), there were exceptions, among them, already in the 15th Century, Joan of Arc standing out, culminating in the figure of the "warrior virgin" (*virgo bellatrix*) of the Classics, scandal for society, and at the same time a motive for exaltation.

Beginning in the 12th Century, the chivalry orders began opening themselves up to women, through help to sick people and hospitality –it suffices to mention the Order of the Hospitable Sisters of Saint John of Jerusalem, founded in the actual Jerusalem, established in Spain in 1188-–.

And there was more: according to the blazonist Crollalanza, the orders of chivalry exclusively for women were rather numerous. They arose as brilliant colors in the forest of heraldry. Thus, in 1149, the Order of the Ladies of Tortosa or the Hatchet is founded. Ramón Berenguer IV, Count of Barcelona is responsible for its founding, as a tribute to those who fought in the defense of Tortosa when battling the Muslims. After different attacks from the Arabs, the city had remained almost without protection and was barely able to resist. While they awaited reinforcements, the women dressed as men and were able to ward off the attack. Berenguer, in gratitude, instituted the abovementioned order for them, and granted them exemptions and social privileges.

More than two centuries later, in 1387, and also in Hispanic territories, John I of Castille created the Order of the Ladies of the Band, to honor those who had helped in the defense of Palencia besieged by the English.

These movements are spread out throughout space. In the 13th Century, in 1233, Loderigo d'Andalo founded the Order of Chivalry of Saint Maria in Bologna, recognized later by Alexander IV in 1261. This was the first chivalric-religious order to recognize the title of *militesse* for women. Sixtus V dissolved it in 1558.

In 1441, in the Low Countries, inspired by Catherine Baw, and in 1445 by Elizabeth and Mary of Hornes, orders were founded that were open exclusively to women of noble lineage who received the title of "chevalière" (female knight).

And again the women warriors: In 1925 Jeanne de Dampierre, countess of Monfort, among whose deeds the defense of Hennebont stands out. With complete armor and on horseback, she mobilized the citizens and led 300 male knights in search of reinforcements, returning with 600.

In 1475 Isabel of Castille was injured, and she also, with armor and wielding a sword, defended her right to the throne on the battlefield.

Catalina Sforza (1462-1509), Duchess of Imola and Forli, commanded the troops of the Castle of Sant'Angelo upon the death of Pope Sixtus VI, in order to defend her territorial patrimony. And when Alexander VI forced the leaders of Romania to hand over their territories to the Holy See, and Cesar Borgia sieged the castle of Forli, she resisted the attacks at the head of 1,000 soldiers, even though she could not prevent its falling. She was beautiful, and it is true that she is the *La dama dei gelsomini,* painted by Lorenzo di Credi (Pinacoteca of Forli).

And who was that Maria of Pozzuoli? Certainly a *virgo bellatrix* ("warrior virgin") ... Petrarch spoke of her to the Cardinal Francesco Colonna, in a letter dated 24 November 1843:

> [...] Of everything I saw today, and to which I refer in this missive, the most relevant has to do with a marvelous woman of Pozzuoli, strong of body and of soul. Her biggest merit is without a doubt the fact that she has been able to remain a virgin while in close contact with men of arms; it is said that soldiers avoided assaulting her not even by laughing, prevented by fear toward her more than from the respect due a woman. In effect, Maria dresses like a warrior and not a girl, she has a strength comparable to that of a veteran; she does not occupy herself with cloth or needles, or mirrors, but instead with arrows, bows and lances; on her face she does not carry the signs of amorous kisses or of lascivious teeth from lovers, but of wounds inflicted in battle; courageously she scorns death. [...] She has fought often alone or in the company of a few soldiers, but for now has always managed to come out victorious in each confrontation. She presents herself furious in the heat of battle, part of the charge, assaults the enemy with courage, and with cunning prepares for the ambushes. With incredible patience she tolerates hunger, thirst, cold, heat, sleep and fatigue.

> Night and day, tireless she wears the armor and rests her body members in the bed or on the shield as if it were a bed. (114-115)

And the remote countries… Queen Tamara of Georgia, who, crowned in 1178, took charge of the weapons, sketched the combat plans and commanded the army. Perhaps there is a remote echo of the character of the Amazon Zahra, Queen of the Caucasus, who appears in *Amadís of Greece*, of Feliciano de Silva, much more distant, despite everything, from the model utilized by Doña Urraca in the ballad. In fact, in some cases, it is by way of the legend that one is able to pull out some thread of the events that time and fantasy have adjusted to the needs of imagination of the moment.

The Archetype

The ideal of the combative and heroic woman, in her two aspects: as a warrior maiden (who, for circumstances, hides her sex and practices chivalry) and an amazon (combative by nature and educated for it from the beginning) arises in the books of chivalry beginning with the text of Arthurian tinges of Heldris of Cornwall, *Romance of Silence* (1270), whose protagonist, Silence, is close to the amazon Camila in *Roman d'Eneas* (*Aeneas' Romance*, 1150-1160), which is inspired at the same time in the amazon of Virgil's *Aenid.*

In the 12th Century, along with the *Roman d'Eneas*, the *Roman de Troie* and the *Roman d'Alexandre* (*Romance of*

Troy, Romance of Alexander) also incorporate that motif. Spanish literature does it in the same way: Amadís introduces the warrior maiden with Calafia, queen of the island of California; *The Chronicle of the Very Valiant and Dedicated Knight Platir* (1533), with Florinda; *Belianís of Greece* (1579), with Hermiliana. In the *Sergas of Esplandián (Adventures of Esplandián)* of Garci Rodríguez of Montalvo (1496?), there appear amazon women. Pedro Laín's Don Silves of the *Jungle* (1549) presents us with nothing less than Pantasilea, and Beatriz Bernal's *Cristabolín of Spain* (1545) with Minerva.

Taking another leap in fantasy: the character Brunilda of Nordic and Germanic mythology has Hispanic origin. Apparently, she was inspired in the historic queen Brunequilda, born in Toledo in the year 546, daughter of the Visigoth king Atanagildo and of Gosuinda, and married to the Merovingian Segisberto I of Austrasia. Before dying, Sergisberto's father, Clotario I, had divided the kingdom ceding Neustria to Chilperico I, lover of the terrible Fredegunda. Both brothers, each aspiring to the throne of the other, and Fredegunda, with murder after murder, were doing away with the Brunequilda family. But Brunequilda was a tenacious warrior, directing the struggle for power among the Francs and, until she was 70, she continued to fight for legitimate succession, first for her children, and then her grandchildren and then finally for her great-grandchildren. Her troubles did not end with the death of Fredegunda, for she had to keep on fighting. Betrayed by one another, the son of her enemy, Clotario II, ended up taking her prisoner, subjecting her to torture and to being dismembered by four horses.

How this Brunequilda of Austrasia, daughter of Atanagildo, became the Brunilda of the *Saga de the Volsungs,* of the *Poetic Edda,* of the *Song of the Nibelungs*, and finally, of Wagner's *Tetralogy*? Without a doubt because of her unbreakable combative character, that soon involved her in legend, while the imagination converted her into a feminine deity at the service of Odin, dweller of Valhala.

Brunilda then, with helmet and breastplate, ends up riding horseback through the air and achieving heroic deeds, if indeed, due to an act of disobedience, she sees herself punished and abandoned to sleep, although surrounded by a ring of fire that only the most valiant hero could cross. That hero will be Siegried and he will, upon removing the helmet from the warrior he has just seen and discovered is a female, become fascinated.

Many centuries before the birth of Brunequilda, in the year 400 B.C., the work *Lisistrata* of Aristophanes was debuted, giving us another face of the woman's struggle, in this case through the sexual strike against the war, which constituted a symbol of the first effort organized in favor of peace. The aforementioned Greek women did not hide their curls under their helmets, but in a certain way their stimulus connected with the heroic spirit of the amazons, whose queen, Pentesilea, completely covered in military garb, helped the Trojans at the end of the war. Beaten by Achilles, and already dead, she had the power to seduce him in the moment he discovered her face. Without a doubt the fact of taking –or taking off– the helmets and of revealing a face "like the sun" and a beautiful mane of hair, accentuates the value of the event in itself along with the surprise element.

There is no surprise. And, on the other hand, the intensity is chilling, in the appearance of the male/female warrior Mahabhárata, the Hindu epic poem whose oldest oral tales could date from the 4th Century B.C. It has to do with, in fact, a woman named Amba, reincarnated in the warrior Sikhandi. The valiant and invincible Bhishma, to whom was conceded the moment of electing his death, swears to stay celibate and to serve whoever is seated on the throne of his father, whoever that might be. It happens later that he kidnaps three princesses in order to marry them to his brother. One of them, Amba, in love with King Salva, begs of him to free her. Bhishma does it instead and she returns to Salva, but he tells her now that her master is her captor and she should marry him. Amba, with tears in her eyes, presents herself before Bhishma, begging him to make her his wife. He, to fulfill his vows, rejects her. Filled with rancor, she leaves for the forest and for 10 years lives in continuous ascesis. Her only desire is to avenge herself and she seeks help, but everyone respects the conquering and celibate leader too much, and no one wants to help her. After many setbacks, Amba is given the chance to reincarnate herself as the male warrior, Sikhandi, who will do away with her kidnapper. The moment of the great combat between the Pandavas and the Kurus arrives. Bhishma, over 100 years of age and still invincible, for having sworn to serve whoever is on his father's throne, sees himself as obligated to fight against descendants of his very same lineage, the Pandavas, who call him grandfather and whom he loves. One of them, Arjuna, one could say has the same strength in battle: he is the only one who could take his life, assuming he accepts dying. Exhausted from so much massacre and conscious that Amba, to whom he caused great harm, has been reincarnated in Sikhandi, Bhishma decides that he will lay down his weapons before a woman. And thus Arjuna will be able to cause his death. This is Bhishma's reflection:

> Amba hates me. I can only think of her as Amba and not as a man, Sikhandi. Arjuno hates me, but between love and hate there is little difference. A small change in point of view and they are the same. She is the person who will grant me freedom from these ties of life that have been imposed on me. I can only rid myself of the burden of this life with Amba's help. Do not doubt, all; place her in front of my carriage. Watching how her eyes fill with hate, I will put down my arms. Arjuno, you should remain behind Amba, and kill me with your arrows; only you can kill me. I assure you that my blessings will rain over you. (118)

New confrontations take place. And "suddenly the sweetest breeze blew over Bhishma" (118). The moment had arrived. Due to his look and his affectionate words, the Pandavas knew that he was ready to die. They carried out the reincarnation of Amba before him. And Sikhandi, "fired five sharp arrows wounding him. Perhaps in her mind Amba was thinking about the five arrows of the love of God". And "Bhishma did not respond to the fight". Then, "Closing his lips rapidly so that sobs did not escape him, Arjuno fired arrow after arrow at the old man who lay in his carriage and had abandoned his bow and arrows". Bhishma dies happy; Sikhandi disappears… (118)

A small change in point of view….

Bibliography

Aranda Torres, C., "La aportación del islam hispano a la caballería medieval vista por Hegel" ("The Contribution of Hispanic Islam to the Medieval Chivalry Seen by Hegel"), *Al Andalus*, No. 249, 1 April 2004.

Cirlot, V., *Hildegard von Bingen y la tradición visionaria de occidente (Hildegard von Bingen and the Western Visionary Tradition)*, Herder, Barcelona, 2005.

Cirlot, V. and B. Gari, *La mirada interior: Escritoras místicas y visionarias en la Edad Media (The Interior Gaze: Visionary and Mystic Women Writers in the Middle Ages)*, Roca, Barcelona, 1999.

Cornualles, H. de, *Libro de Silence* (*Book of Silence*), Madrid, Siruela, 1986.

Gordo Molina, A. G., "Urraca I de León y Teresa de Portugal. Las relaciones de fronteras y el ejercicio de la potestad femenina en la segunda mitad del Siglo XII. Jurisdicción, Imperium y Linaje" ("Urraca I of Leon and Teresa of Portugal. Border Relationships and the Exercise of Feminine Power in the Second Half of the Twelfth Century. Jurisdiction, Imperium and Lineage".). http: //www. medievalismo. org.

Martín Pina, M. C., "Aproximación al tema de la *virgo bellatrix* en los libros de caballería españoles ("Approximation to the Theme of the "virgo bellatrix" in the Spanish Novels of Chivalry"), *Criticón*, No. 45, 1989, pp. 81–94.

Nelli, R., in the first volume of *Escrivains anticonformistes du Moyen-Age Occitan (Anti-conformist Writers in the Western Middle Ages)*, Phébus, Paris, 1977.

Niiranen, S. "Miroir de mérite" ("Mirror of Merit"). Valeurs Sociales, rôles et image de la femme dans les textes mediévaux des trobairitz (Social Values, Roles and Image of the Female in Medieval Texts of the Trobairitz). Iyväskylä Studies in Humanities, 115, https: //www. jyu, fi.

Ortega y Gasset, J., "Introducción" a Ibn Hazm, *El collar de la Paloma* ("Introduction" to Ibn Hazm, *The Ring of the Dove*, Sociedad de Estudios y Publicaciones, Madrid, 1952.

Riquer, M. *La lírica de los trovadores (The Lyric of the Troubadours)*, Escuela de Filología, 1948.

Rougement, D. de, *El amor y Occidente* (*Love in the Western World*), Kairós, Barcelona, 1978.

Rubiera Mata, M. J., "La huella literaria de Al-Andalus" ("The Literary Trace of Al-Andalus"), in *http: //www. cervantesvirtual. com.*

Tavera, S., *Las mujeres y las guerras. El papel de las mujeres desde la Edad Antigua a la Contemporánea. (Women and War. The Role of Women from Ancient to Contemporary Times)*, Icaria, Barcelona, 2003.

VV. AA, *Mujeres de luz. La mística femenina y lo femenino en la mística. (Women of Light. The Female Mystic and the Feminine in Mysticism)*, Trotta, Madrid, 2001.

Vyasa, *Mahabhárata* (*Mahabhárata*), Edicomunicación, Barcelona, 2006.

VI- That Time In Which Queens Were Slaves Or The Disguise

> I wish to entertain myself
> in this way; may it not astonish you
> that I fancy the suit of man as appealing
> since I can not be one.

Who wrote these verses? Not a woman, for sure, but Tirso de Molina, who put them in the mouth of one of the characters of *El vergonzoso en palacio* (*The Shameful in Palace*). In effect, Serafina adopts male dress, but not like other theater heroines to go in search of a lover or to undertake warrior matters, but instead to represent a *comedia* (Renaissance play). It is likely that a woman of that period, the Golden Age in Spain, should also use the word *entretener* ("to entertain"), but the interesting aspect of these verses is not the word itself but the verb that concludes: *puedo ser* ("I can be"). To be able to be or not to be able to be, that is the question, we should say, modifying the Hamletian disjunction. And this "to be able" or not, encloses not the comedy but the tragedy. But the human spirit is capable of taking a turn and presenting it in a humorous manner, including with little suffering. What happens on the inside, nevertheless, forbidden at times to one's own person, is not exactly a reason for laughter. The fact of being female and longing to be a man indicates, at minimum, a discomfort, and that discomfort seeks a way out that is certainly connected to the "power to be", with the "possibility". If the woman wants to be a man, it is because she sees that the man has more "possibilities", for freedom above all (121).

To ask oneself currently for the meaning of the word *freedom*, when a physicist such as Einstein, basing himself on scientific discoveries, affirmed: "Human will is not free... [...] everything is determined by forces over which we have no control"[9], is almost a fantasy. And, given everything, it is enough for us to look back in order to see the relative matter of the question. Whatever may be the degree of freedom that we enjoy, this (freedom) is found, without a doubt, linked to autonomy. And autonomy demands that one act on one's own initiative, and at least, privacy. Now then, in the moment in which Tirso de Molina was writing those verses, even the women of nobility found unlimited obstacles in this regard. In those times, they did not even dream about a room of their own, and perhaps, as paradoxical as it seems, they found in disguise a stronghold where their personality could develop.

Intimate Prisons

In the heart of the Renaissance, Fray Luis de León wrote: "Because just as Nature [...] made women so that, enclosed, they might keep house, and as such also obligated them to shut their mouth" (122). This sentiment dominated in such a natural way that the artist, in many cases, accepted the anonymity. A century later she could take the name of a knight as a pseudonym, as did María of

9 Kaku, M., *Parallel Universes*, Atalanta, Gerona, 2008, p. 184.

Zayas, too powerful a writer not to be a male! The framework was rigid, and it began with the highest estate.

Perhaps the closest thing to slavery is what the protocol imposed on women of noble lineage. It was the so-called ceremony of Burgundy, procedure that was established in said duchy in the middle of the 15th Century. It passed to Spain, via Phillip the Beautiful (son of Burgundy) and with Charles I. Modified later by Phillip II, it was converted into the Spanish label, pointing toward, above all, the "divinization" of the royal family, with the first victim being the queen.

She, even though she lived in her quarters –the king in his– without a doubt and more than anybody, lacked an enclosure for herself. Those quarters consisted of a series of rooms in a row: living room, small living room, antechamber, additional chamber outside, chamber with a podium, inner chamber and chamber "where her Majesty slept" (to which were joined a dresser, with the dresses she had worn then, and a toilet with the elements necessary for her hygiene), but in none of them could the sovereign queen be alone. Controlled incessantly by her ladies, as if "divinized", she was almost untouchable, which she was actually –except when the king visited her– and did not have a moment of true intimacy. Even when she was giving birth, she should do it in public, that is, surrounded by people from the nobility, and before a notary, and in addition, any direct service she would receive from her ladies kneeling before her. These, for their part, were continually under the vigilance of a major guard and a guard.

Each of the royal rooms had a purpose, one could say that acted like a filter –and a wall–distinguishing between the people who could come in and those who could not. The visitors were received in the podium room, where the queen was seated in a chair with a canopy, while her ladies sat on the floor and the men remained standing. When the queen did not eat in public or with the king, she ate in the room furthest out, alone and in silence, served by her ladies, kneeling naturally. In the innermost chamber she was with her ladies and her children. As for the one in which she slept, the only persons to have access were the king, the ladies of honor, her own ladies, and the senior lady-in-waiting, who also spent her sleeping hours there.

There was more: neither the queen or king could dance in plain sight; they had to do it wearing masks and even disguised –"in this way / may it not surprise you"... (123). With such a number of impediments, these "majesties" could easily feel themselves like that character whose senses had been pulled out –since the senses and the world seemed like occasions for evil– from the work *Garden of Falerina*, of Calderón de la Barca, that exclaimed:

> Live statue am I,
> but I have (Ay, unhappy!)
> eyes to not see
> ears to not hear
> lips to not speak,
> feet to not flee,
> to not touch hands,
> to not discourse
> memory.... (124)

But, in fact, it was not so bad, since, in spite of that incarceration that, in the case of the queens, meant being continually in the presence of another, these and other noble women in private enjoyed distractions: concerts, hunting, excursions, visits to convents, and, without the presence of gentlemen, dances, carnivals and theatre performed by women. Now some and then others were allowed to devote themselves to an art. Thus, among the women belonging to the nobility, Juana of Austria, sister of Phillip II and widow of don Juan, principal heir of Portugal, a lover of music, founded the Convent of the Royal Barefooted Nuns and gathered there a notable musical and literary library with numerous paintings; Elisabeth of Valois developed her painting talent; Elizabeth Clara Eugenia followed her literary hobbies, while Anna and Margarita of Austria chose sport and hunting.

And on the other hand, "it does astonish". The following paradox astonishes: it was in the moments when women were not touched when the queen enjoyed the greatest freedom, such that, as regent, she had to make decisions, that is, when, in fact, she assumed the role of the man. The confidence that was granted her in this regard astonishes. Perhaps the explanation lies in that it did not have to do with things related to that fundamental virtue required of the feminine condition, and above all, of noble women: modesty. The painter Sofonisba of Anguissola, who came from Italy to the court of Spain as Elisabeth of Valois' teacher, even though she painted the entire royal family, except for gifts, could never receive payment for her works, nor sign them. As a consequence, they were soon attributed to Sánchez Coello, or to Titian, or to El Greco.

Even today *La dama del armiño* (*Lady of Ermine*) is believed to belong to the latter (El Greco), a private portrait of the Princess Catalina Micaela, sister of Isabel Clara Eugenia, in which there is detected a style typical of the Italian painter, passionate and alive, removed as much from the stylizations of Domenico Theotocópulos, as from the paintings of representation. (And, in fact, how well these paintings represent the historic moment!).

That mix of possibility and impossibility seems to characterize the life of creative women in those times. On one hand, the work in the field of medicine by Oliva Sabuco, who was cruelly plagiarized, was in contrast with the recognized work of María of Zayas and the existence of the "saraos" (feminine equivalent of the "academies"), where theoretical debates took place, novels were enacted or put to dialogue, and contests of music, dance and poetry were held, like in the style of the French "précieuses" (educated women who frequented salons devoted to lively discussions and playful word games).

Blame And Virtue

The first time that a palace "sarao" (soiree) is mentioned is on the occasion of a celebration in the Portuguese court, during Christmas of 1500, of which we are told that a "mask" entertains the queen, and all of it concludes with a dance they call "serau". Then, already in times of Phillip II and Phillip III, the term is used to describe the ceremonial dance of the highest nobility and brings the end to a party. Beginning in 1624, some changes take place and "the courtesan saraos" incorporate and stylize popular dances, while, on the other hand, these dances begin appropriating the term. Finally, they extend to the theatre like a choreographic ritual.

The use of the word "sarao", in the sense of a musical ceremony, figures in the texts of María of Zayas –referring in them to a plot of connections for different narrations– and also, among them, in those of Sor Juana Inés de la Cruz, whether it be poems or plays, like *The Deceits of a House*, and *Love is more Labyrinth*, in order to refer to the poetic script of a spectacle.

In truth, it could be said that, not only on stage but in life, in that "great theater of the world", the nobility could count on their set design and props –those rooms–, and with their choreography: the movement of the ladies and chambermaids, and above all, of the queens, who should abide by that fixing of possibilities concealing the lack of privacy, just as the same idea of being served while kneeling –as we see by Velázquez' painting *Las meninas* (*The Ladies-in-Waiting*).

Naturally, all of them were also subject to the dressing room, another prison that the queen shared with the princesses and other ladies; the chest cardboard, that maintained them upright and without shapes, the childguard who plumped up their skirts, the petticoat, that gave them firmness and amplitude, and the very small shoes that would force them to walk with little steps, and many other details. It seems as if, during this period, every gesture would take place in the shadow of those words that Guilt thrusts at man in *La hidalga del valle* (*The Noblewoman of the Valley*).

> Oh peasants, children of Adam,
> those who are, those who have been
> and who have to be forever
> conceived in sin.
> [...]
> To your nature,
> my slave,
> I bring with me,
> shoed with harsh
> irons that in your face I imprint.
> I am Guilt, I am
> the serpent, of whom
> Moses said in the Genesis,
> walked disguised through Paradise.
> I am that beautiful prodigy
> crowned on a monster
> of seven different necks
> that John saw in the Apocalypse,
> with a glass of rich gold,
> to offer mortal poisons
> of affectionate spells. (126)

The force of guilt, overlapping the present in every moment, prepared, without a doubt, the fact that the kings and queens, after the artifice of the mask, would go sit next to "Virtue".

In a relaying of the parties celebrated in Valladolid in 1605, titled "Sarao that his Majesties organized in the palace for the birth of our prince Señor Sir Phillip" (future Phillip IV), it is said:

> That dance continued with different movements, and lasted a good while with admiration from all those present; and when it was over, the Majesties were carried up to the temple where they sat on two chairs, seated on both sides of Virtue, and removing the masks, the king took up a hat decorated with feathers, which the ladies and gentlemen who wore masks also did, and they watched another dance performed by the six ladies-in-waiting. (127)

But with the removal of the mask, it became clear that as much this as the disguise itself took on a plural significance: to hide and also uncover. And even more: diversion lay under the façade of each. In another telling[10], one reads:

> Couples presented themselves in plain sight, four ladies with brownish black masks, pants and skirts of scarlet satin, garnished in gold, hoop skirts, fleece cloaks, handfans and headdresses of silver, hatchets in their hands. It was the utter serene Queen [and her ladies....], and having danced a while, very lively, in the same evenness, once returned to the dressing room, the second group appeared. [...] the third entered, dressed in blue satin [....]. Having been received equally, they each danced for half an hour with many turns and loops, that were seen with difficulty, but they danced with such skill in everything that, no matter how confusing the sight was for everyone who watched, they finished more arranged in their positions. The Queen guided her mask so artfully and

10 Telling of the famous drama of the *Prize of Beauty and Enamored Love*, that the Prince, our Lord, the very Christian Queen of France and the very Serene Princes Lord Carlos and Lady Maria, their brothers and sisters and some ladies-in-waiting acted out in the Park of Lerma, Monday, 3rd of November, 1614.

> with such care, that even when there was no one to follow her, she would not get lost (127).

Dressed Up And Covered Up

In a period of such complex artifice –where the challenge was "concert" among "confusion"–, theater triumphed and incorporated both the mask and the disguise with spectacular results, lending itself to mistakes and highly comic situations. The female disguises herself as a man either to pursue her lover or to commit violent or intrepid acts, more common for a man. In *The Devotion of the Cross*, of Calderón de la Barca, Julia, who has committed serious crimes, flees from justice by this process; in *The Valiant Céspedes*, by Lope de Vega, María, disguised as a man, encounters Theodora, also with her clothing reversed, and both participate in a battle accompanying the Emperor Charles. In *White Hands Do Not Offend*, of Calderón, one arrives at the height of confusion because many cross-dress and cause confusion. What was, in fact, the secret of this confusion? Perhaps it resided in those verses of *The Shameful in Palace* of Tirso de Molina; in that fancying of that which cannot be.

Undoubtedly a longing for change and freedom, on the part of the female, beats beneath these movements of attire in a period of enormous misogyny, where daring, intelligence, kindness and courage were attributes that were associated only with the male character. Such a way of feeling was based on a tradition that goes back to Aristophanes, who affirms in his *Poetics*: "There can also be a good woman, and a slave, although woman is perhaps an inferior being, and the slave completely vile".

But woman, for the Baroque, is not inferior in its capacity to do evil. Let us pause for a moment with the character Julia, from *The Devotion of the Cross*. Secluded in a convent, she is assaulted by Eusebio, who, after inflaming her, flees upon seeing the cross on her chest. She escapes from the cloister and pursues him, not caring about giving death to a man on the road. The scene is a mountain where Eusebio, some bandits and Julia, dressed like a man and with her face covered, encounter each other. He asks: "Who is that gentleman / whose face is covered?" (128). She demands that they be alone, and when this happens, she says pulling out her sword:

> Julia: So that for once
> you know why I've come,
> and whoever I am, take out your sword;
> for in this way I say
> that I am the one who comes to kill you.
> After a brief dialogue, he alleges:
> I, to defend myself, more
> than to offend you, fight,
> for now your life does not matter to me;
> for if in this challenge
> I kill you, I do not know why:
> and if you kill me, the same for you.
> Show yourself now then,
> if it pleases you.
> She, finally, reveals herself and says:
> Do you know me? Why are you frightened?
> Why are you looking at me?
> Eusebio:

That surrenderedto the truth and to the doubt
in confusing ravings,
I am frightened of what I see,
I am astonished at what I look at. […]
You, Julia, you in this mountain?
You with your profane dress,
twice violent on you?
How have you come here alone?
What is this?
Julia: Your scorns
they are and my disenchantments.
And so that you see that it is an arrow
discharged, burning shot,
fast lightning, a woman
who runs after her appetite,
not only have they given me pleasure
the sins committed
up until now, but they continue
giving it to me, if I might repeat them. (129-130)

No, the backdrop of that deception through disguises was not always comic. Historically, at any rate, to hide under a disguise was always joined with covering oneself, a feminine custom that stemmed from Roman times, since Strabo already mentions that Hispanic women wear a veil that "shades them and covers their face and this works for them as gala and adornment" (130). Basilio Sebastián Castellanos remembers this in the article, "Origin of Veils in Spain", published in 1838, where he also speaks of the Arabic influence. He adds: "In ancient times, Spanish women used veils of two kinds, one that covered the face entirely and another that left one eye revealed" (130).

Going back to Juan de la Puente, when explaining that such a style gave way to the figure of the "covered woman with half an eye", he says: "From the Arabs the Spanish women adopted covering themselves except for half an eye, for which Tertullian praised them" (130). This custom was repeatedly prohibited by the Council of Trent of 1324, since it was considered an assault on honesty. From the beginning, those who converted to Catholicism were called on to stop wearing the "Moorish dress". Those who gave orders to this effect included James I, Queen Joanna, Charles I and Phillip II. And Castellanos goes on in the article quoted below:

The Arabs managed to continue compromising with the law until the terrible and inhumane decree of Phillip II published in Granada in 1566, and that prepared another one even more atrocious yet. From this period on, the Arabic women wore skirts and shawls and began to cover themselves with these completely except for half an eye such as they also did with the "malafas"[11]. Spanish women, from way back, always attuned to accenting their gracefulness, began to see that the covered Moorish women wore their shawls displayed in the proudest way, and with their beautiful eye stole the attention of the gallant knights, took on the covering up as fashion and became confused with the Moorish women, which allowed them daily conquests, such that fortunately in 1567 the complete covering up was introduced into Spain with the exception of Navarre and the Basque provinces [...]. The covering began to be abused to such an extent that its prohibition was discussed in the Courts of Madrid of 1586, and in 1590

11 *Malafa*, Arab dress that covered from the shoulders to the feet.

a law was published that, as the first, was reproduced in the statutes in 1594, and then in 1600 a compilation was added, and then finally that of 1639 that prohibited the veil entirely under terrible penalties.

The veil was one of the reasons for the revolution of the Moriscos from Granada. [… Their use] was forbidden in Spain from 1639 up to the end of the 18th Century, when it was introduced again by the French Dynasty, more tolerant with this kind of material, if not as a mantle to cover one's face then as a headdress ornament; but as the century went on the Spanish women were mocking a law and somewhat ridiculous by now, and adding the veil to their head-coverings. (130-131)

Not always, then, for sometimes women desired male dress, but then according to intent.

In the theater, the women would appear showing off the whole realm of possibilities, not only showing themselves as travesties, but also covered (and the men in capes); and the works that depended on this confusion were numerous, such as Calderón's comedy of Cape and Sword: *The Hidden Male and the Covered Female* (*El Escondido y la tapada*). There were authors, nevertheless, who did not take advantage of these situations in order to cause laughter but who sought instead the bloody deceit, such as Quevedo, who brutally treats those "eyes set in puffs[12] –he says– that enable women to provoke love with eyes like bridges, and allowing them to come in" (131). This phrase belongs to his

12 Type of very fine mantle, made out of very light taffeta in such a way that it allowed one to see precisely what was covered.

Life of the Court and Trades Entertained in it and Role of the Common Things in Court as by Alphabet", and its ending referred to the licentious conduct of some women. Such it is that, as in the case of the disguise, covering oneself up had the ultimate goal of allowing one to be seen.

Crows Of The Convents

All of this is situated clearly within the Baroque *topos* of the "world in reverse", and besides, it is a way of transgressing the established order, and, on behalf of the dramatists, of awakening the spectator as regards the social panorama of the time, in support of the woman and her rights: but is this an honest support or also an artifice? For Natalia Seseña, it is the "awakening of the female to modernity. A slow awakening". She says this in the article "Life in Cloister", when commenting on the description of the "female gallant ones" that Lucas Fajardo mentioned in 1603: "unfocused and disheveled, that allow entry and bring visits, wearing the mantle on their shoulder" (132).

In this world of paradoxes, it is not surprising that it was behind the closed convent door where many women would find a "way out". "The cloister –as Seseña affirms– for the majority of friars and nuns, was a career, a profession, a way out". And she adds: "There were many endowed with intelligence, wisdom, and intellectual curiosity, who preferred the convent society to be able to listen to ideas espoused by their confessors or written in books, to being only, and with enough frequency, women-mothers not taken into account in civil society or hungry for enriching dialogues" (132).

In the convent, then –there existed a tradition in this regard, whose most relevant example is Saint Teresa– that woman was sheltered and did have possibilities of developing her intellectual aptitude. Nuns who were authors were numerous, important personalities such as Sor Juana Inés of la Cruz, Sor Marcela of San Fénix, or María Jesús of Agreda. This latter one, correspondent for Phillip IV for 22 years, was able to write and publish her "Mystic City of God: " "spiritual, scriptural and theological dictates" (María Pilar Panero), if indeed the work was included on the index of forbidden books, although only briefly (132).

Sor Marcela of San Félix, daughter of Lope de Vega and of the comic "La Barrera" (Micaela de Luján), joined the Convent of the Barefoot Trinitarians in Madrid at the age of 16, since she, because she was an illegitimate daughter, had few possibilities of contracting a good marriage. Endowed in letters, she demonstrated ability in her theater and poetry, she criticized with humor the weaknesses of daily life in the cloister, and she dealt with a wide thematic gamut, having recourse to biblical topics and to the use of allegory as much for the conflicts as for the ideal of religious life. Her handling of the carol is firm. This is the beginning of the one she wrote "To the profession of the Sister Isabel of the Saintly Sacrament: "

> Love could not make
> your happiness greater.
> Today when you offer your soul, Isabel,
> to the happiest union

> and from your spouse you deserve
> the sweet mental embrace,
> and to his divine lap
> you surrender your beautiful April,
> for in order to make it gentle
> such a frequent flower,
> love could not
> make your happiness greater. (133)

Among other women writers the following stand out, Sor María of Santa Isabel, from the royal convent of the Conception, fertile poet, who used the pseudonym of Marcia Belisarda, and Ana Francisca of Abarca and Bolea, superior of a monastery of the Cistercian Order, who was the author of the beautiful sonnet, "At the death of Prince Balthasar", that figures in the *Historic Obelisk, honorarium that the Imperial City of Zaragoza erected to the memory of the Most Serene Señor Don Balthasar Carlos of Austria, Prince of Spain*. Luisa Manrique also ended up in the convent: She first entered the service of Queen Isabel, wife of Phillip IV, contracted marriage with don Manuel Manrique of Lara, Count of Paredes, and having become widowed, took charge of the education of the princesses, and after, joined the Barefoot Carmelites with the name Luisa Magadalena of Jesús.

There were those who, on the other hand, did not need to close themselves up, such as Cristobalina Fernández of Alarcón, the "Sybil of Antequera" –as Lope calls her in the "Laurel of Apollo"– the one who, because she was a natural daughter, was not obliged to take the habit, and with her father being a scribe, learned grammar and letters. She was married twice, and besides, also unleashed the passion of the poet Pedro of Espinosa, and it was he who, after her second marriage, retired to a hermitage. Winner of jousts and poetic contests, on the other hand, very few of her poems remain, among them this sonnet to the Battle of Lepanto:

> From dust the smoke ascends to the heavens,
> the heavens seek out their sphere, and meanwhile
> Neptune looks with terror and fright
> his Cerulean veil bathed in blood.
> To the very deep center of the earth
> descend a thousand souls in eternal weeping
> to relate the battle of Lepanto,
> and others fly to the realm of consolation;
> when Charles the valiant son,
> Spanish Scipion, triumphant Cesar,
> lifting up his memory with his deeds:
> "Virgin, Lady of the Rosary, he said,
> Conquer our enemy!" –and in an instant
> the victory by the Christians was pronounced. (134)

Precisely Pedro of Espinosa ordered the poems of the book *Illustrious Flowers of Spain*, published in Valladolid in the year 1605, in which the following beautiful sonnet by Hipólita of Narváez is included:

> My sunshine left, and the storm came
> (but I do not expect less of her absence),
> and the turquoise sky covered up its
> serene eyes, obliged from the discord.
> A very sad tone bursts out
> among the winds, full of clouds;
> the clouds tremble with their husky thunderbolts,

the fields burn, fear grows greater.
The sun came out and dressed its East
in golden jaspers, and the mountains and
flat lands in fine emeralds;
it embroidered the shadowy clouds with strands of gold,
the oak trees oozed blond honey
and the blue mountains white milk. (134-135)

Nor was the work of Leonor of the Cueva and Silva collected; some of her verses are preserved in the National Library in Madrid, as is her dramatic work "Firmness in Absence". She was, apparently, the niece of Don Francisco of the Cueva and Silva, extravagant poet and fan of astrology, which brought on him not a few problems and even a judicial trial. Born in Medina del Campo, Leonor never moved from her birthplace. Among the poems that have reached us is this very characteristic sonnet of the period:

I do not know if I am dying or if I live,
I am not within myself, nor can I find myself outside,
nor in such oblivion can I care to seek myself,
for I am dressed in pain and sorrow.
It gives me sorrow to see myself abhorred
and, if they love me, I end up not pleasing myself;
nothing can make me happy,
everything makes me mad and leaves me tasteless:
I do not abhor, nor do I love, nor do I stop loving,
nor do I stop loving, nor do I love, nor do I abhor,
I do not live confident or jealous;
that which I scorn and at times adore and love,
I seem a varying portent of a condition,
for everything human tires me. (135)

Overseas, among others, the well-known Peruvian Amarilis (María de Rojas y Garay, 1594-1622), a nun who, apparently, left the cloister in 1617, admirer of Lope de Vega, she wrote and addressed to him the known *Epistle to Balardo*, that was published in *The Nightingale (La Filomena),* for which Lope himself wrote the introductory sonnet for her:

> Amaryllis sings, and her voice lifts up
> my soul from the orbit of the moon,
> to the intelligences, for none
> imitates hers with as much sweetness. (136)

It remains, then, clear that during that time women were given to write, even though their poems, in general, have been lost or are only found in songbooks ("cancioneros") or laudatory books in homage to the memory of an important person, resulting clearly superior those subjected to the sonnet "corset".

The nuns' writings underwent a different kind of fate, for they were preserved in convents. Nevertheless, they were not liberated either, in many cases, from anonymity and something worse: the manipulation and theft of the writings. It happened that the same confessors and priests, who had encouraged them to annotate their biographies or chronicles, well protected by their black cassocks, watched them like crows, appropriated their texts, submitted them to a final revision and then signed them. So then, even from within the convent, the intellectual freedom of the cloistered women was deceptive: they suffered corrections, modifications, and thievery, besides the threat from the Inquisition, which watched incessantly to see if they adapted to the established moral and religious principles.

Under The Volcano

Not even Juana of Asbaje, that is, Sor (Sister) Juana Inés of the Cross, was liberated from this type of coercion since, after the writing of the *Athenagoric Letter*, she was considered as hardly devout by the ecclesiastic hierarchies. In her last years (she died in 1695), Sor Juana was the object of a trial overseen by the Bishop Aguiar y Sejias –ready to punish harshly her "religious error"–, and she ended up renouncing and declaring herself the "worst of all women". As a penance, she was required to abandon public life and not to edit her writings. In spite of that, the Phoenix of Mexico and Minerva of America had achieved too much fame already for her name to disappear. The ashes born from the Inquisitorial eruption did not reach her, although its consequences –renouncing her own self and the harsh corporal punishments that brought on a grave illness– ended her life.

The threat of natural catastrophes, may they be volcanos, rains, is present in the Mexican space, and precisely, around Sor Juana's difficult years, there were wind storms and floods and a famine so severe that it provoked riots and accentuated her isolation. Without support of any kind, the nun saw herself driven to negate her past life and to disconnect herself from all books and objects –but notes

Octavio Paz– she did not renounce her poetry. That rooting in her own song, must have had something to do with the land, for the Aztecs established a connection between the poem and the cosmic order, such that they even had a school, the Calmécac, where poets would learn technique with perfection. Some women dominated this art. Hence, in that same passage where the verses of Sor Juana resounded, before the discovery, in times of Axayácatl, Aztec King during the years 1460-1479, there was also heard the voice of a Náhuatl woman poet, the princess Macuilxóchitl, name that means "5-Flower", which could indicate her birthdate. She was the daughter of Tlacaélel, a high military advisor, and she was not the only woman with a nickname among the Aztecs for competing with the men in intellectual questions. With war and religion being the maximum objectives of the State, they found themselves at the foundation of education, with studies of astronomy and the calendar. In the following poem, the victories of Axayácatl are praised, and not at the end as happens in other traditions, but at the beginning, and its author mentions herself:

> I raise my songs,
> I, Macuilxóchitl,
> and with them I please the Giver of Life,
> and may the dance begin!
> To where one exists in some manner,
> to the house of God,
> are the songs taken?
> Or are your flowers
> only here?,
> and may the dance begin!
> The "matlazinca"
> is your gift from your peoples, Señor Itzcóatl,

> you conquered Axayacatzin!
> the city of Tlacotépec! (137-138)

Later she continues mentioning victories:

> Axayácatl everywhere
> made conquests
> in Matlazinco, in Malinalco,
> in Ocuillan, in Tequaloya, in Zohcotitlan.
>
> Around here he emerged again.
> There in Xiquipilco an Otamian
> wounded Axayáctal in the leg,
> his name was Tlílatl. (138)

The conclusion of the poem, curiously, allows us to see the influential and combative role of women: having carried the aggressor to the presence of the king, they defend him:

> The Otamian was afraid,
> and said:
> "Truly they will kill me!"
> He then brought a thick piece of wood
> and the skin of a deer.
> With this he showed reverence to Axayácatl,
> The Otamian was full of fear.
>
> But then his women
> made pleas to Axayácatl on his behalf. (138)

The active gestures of women in Aztec society, that can be discerned from this poem, in the opinion of Francisco Antolín, "anticipates for us what will be the presence of women soldiers in the battlefields" (138).

This is the movement inherited two centuries later by Sor Juana, which –leaving aside her tragic end– manifested itself in her life and in her work, whose strength and perfection remain unscathed, as can be seen for example through the sonnet –in a tone, certainly, very different from Macuilxócitl's poem– titled "Introducing a gallant young man scorned by his lady, complaining of her cruelty: "

> Enough scorn and enough rigors:
> Clori, no more cruelty, no more anger,
> make your divine eyes more serene
> and suspend those killing rays.
> May scorns cease, and disfavors too,
> for it is not good that thistles take the place of flowers
> to he who surrenders his soul to you for remains,
> is not unworthy of enjoying your favors.
> Oh, ungrateful Clori, Oh, ungrateful, that to my complaints
> you have the soul and chest of a diamond,
> and it seems that you live through my death!
> Oh, cruel Clori, although you leave me suffering,
> and even though you kill me, I must be constant,
> fighting against your scorn until I conquer you. (139)

Born in San Miguel de Nepantla in Mexico in 1651, natural daughter of the Spanish military man Manuel of Asbaje y Vargas, Sor Juana learned Náhuatl, with some neighbors, and at three began to read and write, secretly following the lessons of her older sister. She soon discovered her grandfather's library and read everything there was there: classical Greeks, Romans and theology. Her desire to know caused her to conceive the idea of disguising herself as a man in order to attend the university, but they sent her to live in Mexico City with some aunts and uncles who introduced her in the Court, and she served as a lady for the Vice-queen, the Marchioness of Mancera. She wrote poems and showed off a great deal of intelligence, calling the attention of the Viceroys' confessor, Nuñez de Miranda, who, knowing her to be opposed to marriage, persuaded her to profess. She tried it first in the Carmelite order, but her health was too delicate for its rigors. She finally entered the convent of the Jerónimas, where she had servants and a two-floor cell. Always united by friendship with the female Viceroys, she carried on a brilliant intellectual life, until she became involved in that theological dispute that caused her to be considered "not very devout". Her genius, nevertheless, was not up for discussion. She was comparable to a Quevedo, a Lope or a Góngora. She dominated a great variety of genres, registers and themes, and like all of the masters, wrote love poems, mythological and religious ones, of praise and ingenuity –including brilliant acrostics, double and triple, labyrinths and enigmas– to prove the ingenuity of the public. Just like the dramatists, she wrote dramas, one-act religious plays, short theatrical plays of praise and carols. And, following their talent, she defended the right of woman to study and to write, and de fended herself from attacks she had received through various letters, among them the already mentioned *Athenagoric*, the *Answer to Sor Filotea*, and the *Letter of Seraphina* (hiding between this pseudonym in the last dark times of her life).

In the ambitious poem, *First Dream*, where she follows literary tradition since the Ciceronian one of *Scipion's Dream*, in which Dante was also inspired –up until her days, where she presents the soul crossing the universe at night in pursuit of the sense of all creation. The nun's wide intellectual interests, a reader of hermetic works, such as the *Great Art* of Athanasius Kircher, who possessed musical, mechanical and scientific instruments, that she kept in her cell and that, without a doubt, she handled, and they passed to her writings and verses in the form of metaphors: compass, magnet, ("of the air" or lung), clock ("human", the heart) ... This imagery does not cease to surprise us, nor those acrostics or intricate labyrinths either.

LABYRINTO HENDECASYLLABO,

Para dar los años la Exc.ma Señora Condeſa de Galve, al Exc.mo Señor Conde ſu Eſpoſo.

Leeſe tres vezes, empezando la leccion deſde el principio, ò deſde qualeſquiera de los dos ordenes de rayas.

AMante ------ Caro, ------ Dulce Eſpoſo mio,
Feſtivo, y --- Prompto --- Tus felizes años
Alegre -------- Canta ------- Solo mi cariño,
Dichoſo, ------ Porque ------ Puede celebrarlos.
Ofrendas -------- Finas -------- A tu obſequio ſean
Amantes ------ Señas ------- De fino holocauſto.
Al pecho ------ Rica ------- Mi corazon, Joya,
Al cuello ------ Dulces ------ Cadenas mis brazos
Te enlazen ------- Firmes, ---- Pues mi Amor no ignora,
Vfano -------- Siempre, --- Que ſon à tu agrado
Voluntad, ---- Y ojos ------ Las mejores Joyas
Aceptas ----- Solas -------- Las de mis halagos.

No altivas ------- Sirvan ----- No en demonſtraciones
De iluſtres ---- Fieſtas ------ De altos aparatos,
Lucidas ------- Danças ----- Celebres feſtines,
Coſtoſas ------ Galas ------ De Regios Saraos.
Las cortas ------- Mueſtras --- Del cariño acepta,
Victimas ------ Puras ------- Del afecto caſto
De mi Amor -- Pueſto, ---- Que te ofrezco Eſpoſa
Dichoſa ------- La que ---- Dueño te conſagro.
Y ſuple ---------- Porque ----- Si mi obſequio humilde
Para ti -------- Viſto ------- Pareciere acaſo,
Pido, que ------ Cuerdo ----- No aprecies la ofrenda
Eſcaſa, y ------ Corta ------- Sino mi cuydado.
Anſioſo ---------- Quiere ----- Con mi propria vida
Fino mi ------- Amor ------ Acrecentar tus años
Felizes, ------- Y yo ------ Quiero: Pero es vna
Vnida ------- Sola ------- La que anima à entrambos
Eterno ------------ Vive ------- Vive, y yo en ti viva,
Eterna ------ Para que --- Identificados,
Parados ------- Calmen --- El Amor, y el tiempo
Suſpenſos ---- De que ---- Nos miren milagros.

"Hendecasyllable Labyrinth" (141)

(To celebrate the years, the very excellent Lady Countess of Galve to the
very excellent Lord Count, her husband:
Read three times over, starting the lesson from the beginning, or from any of the two orders of strokes

Lover, — — dear one — — , sweet husband of mine
festive and — — soon — — your happy years
joyous — — sing — — only my love.
happy — — because — — you can celebrate them.
Offerings — — fine — — may they be to your gift
lovers — — signs — — of a fine holocaust,
with my heart, like a jewel — — rich — — on my chest,
around my neck — — sweet — — my arms like chains.
May they embrace you — — firm, — — for my love does not ignore
proud — — always, — — they are for your pleasure
freedom — — and eyes — — the best jewels,
you accept — — by themselves — — the jewels of my flattery.
Not haughty — — may they serve, — — no, not in demonstrations
of illustrious — — parties, — — elegant artifacts,
lucid — — dances- — — celebrated parties,
costly — — galas — — of royal "saraos".
You cut them — — symbols- — — of the love accept
victims — — pure from — — the chaste affection
of my love, — — since — — what I offer you happy
wife, — — which, — — master, I devote to you,
supple, — — because — — if my humble gift
for you, — — seen — — it might seem perhaps,
I ask that, — — sane, — — you not appreciate the offering
as scarce and — — short, — — but rather my care.
Anxious — — it wants — — with my own life
my fine — — love — — to grow your happy
years, — — and I — — want, but it is one
united, — — alone — — that which animates both of us.
Eternal — — it lives: — — it lives, and I in you may I live
eternal, —so that — — identified,
stalled — — may they calm — — love and time
suspended — — so that — — miracles may gaze upon us.)

Even though, at the end of her life, she had to give up everything, Sor Juana continued to raise herself up in the field of letters like a bastion, the flames of her poetic verb never saw themselves darkened. Other times, on the other hand, they have been completely erased from the literary horizon. Hence, of the writer Isabel Rebeca Correa, a Sephardic Jew based in Amsterdam, that, we are told had great talent, all of her poems have been lost, except for a composition of circumstances, of which there only remains one translation – very well known in its day– of *The Shepherd Fido*, of Guarini. Highly versed in liberal arts, she created an academy for the more ingenious scholars of the area.

Incestuous Mask

In the field of science, I have already mentioned Oliva Sabuco. To her is owed the discovery of the cerebral fluid which she named "quilo", a discovery that English doctors, because of their relationship with Phillip II and the island, already knew and adopted without mentioning it. Oliva collected her wisdom in a book titled *New Philosophy of the Nature of Man, not known or achieved through the great ancient philosophers*. She dedicated her work to the king and it was published in Madrid in 1587, and reedited with some "amendments" in 1728, by the doctor Martín Martínez, who, on making it clear that if Columbus had erased the *non plus ultra*, Lady Oliva "had the courage to write a new system of medicine", and with it, conquered "the columns that Aristotle and Galeno had set as the final goal of their truths" (142). Besides, as Martínez observed: "There are people who say that this work was not done by a woman; I am persuaded that yes, because the king to whom she dedicated it was too serious and circumspect, such that in a matter as important and serious, nobody would dare to speak to him in disguise" (142). The existence or not of such a "disguise", of such a "mask", continues to raise hackles among the erudite.

Lady Oliva, in her "Dedicatory Letter to Phillip II", placed the book in his protection, for she considered it a great service. Getting ahead of Freud, she affirmed that in her work she "provided a doctrine to know oneself and for man to understand himself and his nature and the natural causes for which he lives and falls ill", causes that had root in the relationship of health with the body and spirit (142-143). And she added that she had discovered all of that without any studies of medicine. In the same letter, she begged the President of the Council of State for protection against those who envied her or were detractors, and that he grant her the favor of "always ordering wise men to gather [...], whom I will try out and give evidence how both things are wrong and have deceived the world, and that the great philosophy and true medicine is contained in this book" (143). Although nothing indicates that this public exam actually took place, Oliva was valued in her time. Sometime later, nevertheless, the book was taken as the work of a man, when the writings of her father were discovered, for it was her own father who tried to take charge of her authorship, apparently moved by his second wife, who had decided to appropriate any benefit she could derive.

Oliva, born in Alcaraz (Albacete) in 1562, contracted matrimony at the age of 18. When she was 25, the *New Phi-*

losophy was published. That same year her father, druggist and high school graduate, conceded power, by means of a decree, to his oldest son Alonso, in order to have the book printed in Portugal, revealing that he, and not his daughter, was the author. After a year, he granted a statement affirming that he was the author of *New Philosophy*, although "I did put and again put as author the name of the already mentioned Luisa of Oliva my daughter, only to give her renown and honor", denying her the earnings (143). These facts cause us to think that there were hidden reasons that induced his daughter to write the "*Letter of Dedication*", where, besides asking for protection, she compared herself with the captive woman Getulia, mentioned by Plinius, whom the lions protected in her escape. It is not hard to imagine that she also found herself in a situation of captivity and fled from it, as well as from a dispute with her father over the authorship of the book. In this battle she came out victorious, including even many years later in 1622, for when her brother Alonso published the work in Portugal, he had to do it with the name of Oliva, since her father could not take away from her the privilege conceded to her by the king, "for all the days of her life" (143).

José Pascual Buxó, in his article "Oliva Sabuco of Nantes", delicately observes that she "would have frecuented the tertulias in which her father, the Doctor Heredia, her godfather from baptism, the poet Juan of Sotomayor, and other provincial witty men ... would discourse periodically about subjects related to moral and natural philosophy and, in particular, to medicine. The young woman would stand out in those meetings not the least because of her intellectual lucidity as for her literary competence, with such luck that –as a consequence of and preference for what was discussed at those meetings– it would fall to her to edit or proofread the treatises that would later make up the *New Philosophy of Man*" (144). On the other hand, Paxual Buxó affirms that the work has a reformist character and that it was probably she who considered that the physiological and medical doctrines that were being propagated should be discussed relating the spirit with the body, and from there he could defend Oliva as the true author.

The *New Philosophy of Man* is composed of seven treatises in dialogue form although at times monologue prevails. In one of them, "True Philosophy and true medicine, hides the ancient ones", it is affirmed that the doctor ought to comfort the patient and liberate his/her brain with "opportune words", so that fear and sadness would disappear, for in the brain are found "the root, the cause and beginning and host of the good and bad juice, of sicknesses and health" (144). Oliva considers that the first of the remedies is the knowledge of oneself on the part of man, whether it be for lack of harmony or for contrast between the actions of the soul and those of the body, as happens in death, for causing the fall of the "native dampness", that is, radical. The disordered affections that, she opines, provoke the fall of the *pia mater*, that brings with it "all of the good juice that it had as food and practice; and as falls that juice such fall all the spirits" (144).

An exemplary fighter, in a period of so many contrasts between light and shadows, Oliva Sabuco deserved without a doubt the synonyms that her contemporaries gave her: "heroic matron", "the honor of Spain", and "tenth muse", this last one granted by Lope de Vega in his one–act religious play, *The Prodigal Son*.

Feminism As Bait

Very different is the case of María of Zayas and Sotomayor, although, as we have seen, also as regards her a disguise was suspected, when it was insinuated that under that name there hid a man. It does not appear that this made her literary career more difficult at all; her works underwent 14 editions throughout the century and the one following.

To prohibit the female signature, and to say that behind the women's names those of male writers are hidden, was also without a doubt, a fashion. Cervantes, in the same prologue of *Don Quixote of the Mancha*, led one to believe that it was a habitual practice, and, in a fake dialogue, wrote: "Also my book must lack in sonnets at the beginning, at least sonnets whose authors were dukes, marquises, counts, bishops, noble ladies or celebrated poets. Although if I asked for them from two or three officials who are friends, I know that they would give them to me, and such that not even those of greater renown in our Spain would be equal to them" (145).

Then the person to whom he directed his comments responded: "The first thing you notice about the sonnets is that they are missing something at the beginning, whether it be characters, major ones, and with a title, which can be fixed if you spend some time composing them, and then you can baptize them and give them the name you wish, bequeathing them immediately with such names as Priest John of the Indies or the Emperor of Trapisonda, for whom I know there is information that they were famous poets, and if they had not been and there might be other pedants and students behind you biting you and murmuring about this truth, may they not give you two "maravedís", for once they find out the lie, they will not cut off the hand with which you wrote them" (145). On the other hand, Cervantes himself, has just opened his work with a prologue of laudatory poems to his characters, among whom figure two supposedly written by a woman, two women of course of fiction: Urganda the Unknown and Lady Oriana.

Similar attitudes, very dispersed, resulted ambiguous and were a gesture that functioned in a different way with a male or female reader. Monika Bosse, in her article, "The Sarao of María of Zayas and Sotomayor: A Reason (Feminine) for Narrating Love", after analyzing the two volumes of *Amorous and Exemplary Novels*, which appeared in 1537 and 1647 respectively, and especially her prologues, affirms that one must see "in its stylistic and thematic variety", the reflection of an *ironic* desire to represent, surpass and parody the ease of the same contemporary literature 'of consumption.' " Speaking concretely about the Second Part, she says: "Continuing the reflections of the author, the violence of their plots causes the surprising impression as if the work had a function that was in first place commercial". And commenting on the side text, "Love, the God of Death: An automaton of the Male Honor", she affirmed: "Thus, the most dramatic events narrated in this exposition or internal frame from the *Amorous and Exem-*

plary Novels of María of Zayas, are 'undeceiving, ' or perhaps also trivialized, from so many other 'model' constellations situated in the arsenal of the moral ideals of the educated public of the time" (The absolute enigma that surrounds the life and work of María of Zayas, Bosse concludes, can be due to the fact that perhaps a woman "might consider her literary activities as a pastime". In this case there must have existed a personal reason or something serious of a political-religious nature that would make difficult the disclosure of the most minimal biographic detail having to do with the famous author" (145-146).

In effect, one can also detect a nod, at the same time ironic and complicit, in Zayas' prologue to the 1637 edition, where she expresses concern over the worry that her novels could be scorned for having come from a female pen: "Who doubts, my reader, that it might cause you astonishment to learn that a woman would have the clarity not only to write a book but also to put her stamp on it [....] who doubts, I say again, that there will be many who attribute this virtuous daring to get my writings out to craziness, being a woman, for in the opinion of many stupid people, it's the same as something incapable" (146). That tone does not diminish. In the *Punished Innocence*, we read: "Why, vain legislators of the world, do you tie our hands for vengeance, making our forces impossible with your false opinions, for you deny us arms and letters? Is our soul not the same as that of men? If the soul is what gives courage to the body, who obliges our men to such cowardice? And I assure that, if you understood how we make fun of you, in order to have us submissive since birth, you are weakening our strength with fears of honor, and the understanding that with the timidity of shame, giving us spinning wheels instead of swords and pillows for books" (146-147).

In the same way that she had done since the mid-15th Century, the nun Teresa of Cartagena, author of *Grove of the Sick*, who wrote *Wonder at the Works of God*, advocating for the originality of her work and her intellectual capacities, María de Zayas, by means of this procedure favored by the time, defends her work and fame, at the same time as woman's honor. She believes that, behind the education given to those of her sex, which ties their hands and feet, is hidden man's fear of female competence. "In the same way that I am not off track in that men of fear and envy deprive woman of arms and letters, as the Moors do to the Christians obliged to serve where there are women, and make them eunuchs in order to be sure of them". "Souls are neither women or men", she will say on another occasion (147).

Notable changes had been produced in society since the days of St. Teresa, and a nun endowed with great wisdom, a teacher, but cloistered in a monastery, was not the same as an educated woman with a sharp ingenuity directing the movements of a salon. Much less if she raised up the level of professionalism and announced her purposes. In this sense, María of Zayas insisted that her intention was "to relate a true case, that would not only serve to entertain but also to announce" (147). Now then, this type of declarations was a topic that responded to the lack of confidence in the moment toward fiction, the same thing that induced Cervantes to say: "Even the lie is better the more it appears to be true" (147).

The Carnival And Power

María de Zayas' *Amorous and Exemplary Novels* (but not Cervantes' *Exemplary Novels*) have concomitances with Boccacio's *Decameron*, very well read in those days, even though they figured in the index of forbidden books. It is not provincial that in 1638 they would appear with the subtitle: *Spanish Decameron*. The second part, on the other hand, would be subtitled by the author herself as *Honest and Entertaining Soirée*. With that, Zayas made clear that her writing was not related to the erudite Italian tendency, but rather to the Spanish tradition of entertaining, more or less popular, where satire was an element of laughter. In this second part, the "soirée" resurges as a courtesan variation of the "carnival of women", a day of the year when women could playfully take over the city. From the disguise then, there was no escape.

And yes, Zayas' writing is related to the carnival techniques more appropriate of the Baroque literature that forms part of the "world in reverse". María Rosa Scaramuzza Vidoni, referring to the *Quixote*, mentions, as common elements, giants, devils, or the pair Lent-Carnival, and also the "crazy—sane or foolish discrete person, the popular courts, the enthronement of a crazy or peasant person, the country wedding, and besides, parodic prophecies, masks, disguises, etc.. In these –she says– the utopic dimension of the common values often emerges (although only in a moment of festivities) and poor people over the powerful ones and crazy ones over the so-called normalcy" (148). And further on, she warns: "One cannot suppose, as does Bajtin, that the Carnivalesque events would be felt or lived as in Medieval times. These events are appropriated by the dominant classes, the aristocracy, the urban bureaucracy, for a diversion based on the scorn of the people of the pueblo". For that reason, the carnival has been transformed she says, citing E. Cros, into an object "to contemplate" and a "factor of discrimination" (148).

These questions are also latent in one way or another in María of Zayas. Now then, if in the first part of her *Novels*, the image of a salon with an Arcadian character prevails, the second, in the words of Monika Bosse: "consists of an authentic 'Court of the 'Just' [Feminine] Revenge". "Love, she says, as a means of 'interior conquest' in Zayas' work, substitutes for, according to the author's critical affirmation, military service undertaken by the nobility. Men's operations are warrior strategies, whose only objective is the conquest of the female in the military sense of occupation and destruction" (148–149).

Such a change in tone is due, without a doubt, to the serious economic and social crisis that was crossing Spain, that brought restrictions with it and kept it apart from the "Renaissance idylls". These were the times of the last phase of the 30-Year War, and of the rivalry of Holland and England for the colonies of the New World. After the Carmelite reform sponsored by St. Teresa and the Council of Trent, those years in which convents were places of social and cultural exchange housing women ascetes as well as victims of a seducer or husband, seemed very remote. Now, a step backward in the opening up, carried with it a return to previous structures. Zayas, observes Alicia Yllera, "returns to a literary model already surpassed, the instructive 'exemplum, ' and gives it new life with a strong personality and impassioned defense of women, relating even the Spanish decadence to the scorn and disrespect for the feminine sex" (149).

If that had too much weight, it was due to everything it represented, in fact a principle of the withdrawal of the mystery of life, a permitting a total upturning of the values and deceit, everything oriented not to a "a power" but to the power, which affected society. The feminine characters, the models to be imitated, were false, just as the Dianas and their knights had been false in their day. The former ideal feminine protagonists: nymphs, amazons or female shepherds, simple archetypes, in the novel of the Golden Age, became unfortunate characters, who rarely achieved their purposes. And all of them were supported by certain existing stereotypes: the mythological, the established image of the need for protection, the subjection of the married woman and, by contrast, "the repentant female sinner" or the "silly virgin". The Arcadian fiction, that constituted a new form of expressing feminine revindication, by situating itself in a moment previous to the "fall" and to the "guilt", and projecting itself toward utopia, was modified in the Counter Reformation. And thus, in *Galatea*, Cervantes' pastoral novel, some disillusioned and indifferent female shepherds appear, an anticipation of Marcela from the *Quixote.*

The Disguises Of Freedom

This also indicates to us a form of covering up very much in agreement with so much dressing and so much apparatus. It happens that what is emerging hidden between the hoopskirts and the pompous headdresses generates among the contemporary males a certain angst that translates into insistence on misogyny. Quevedo, very directly, attacks with harsh irony, and, as María Grazia Profeti observes, he writes "verses like exorcism", moved by "a disturbing feminine phantom" (150). Cervantes, more subtly, can introduce Marcela, a female shepherd who is not really that but instead "the daughter of William the Rich", orphaned of both father and mother, educated and "guarded with much caution and much enclosure" by a priest uncle, and, being so beautiful that "nobody looked at her and who did not bless God", rejects all proposals for marriage (150). And behold that one day, the "prissy one", –says Ambrosio, the story's narrator– appeared "turned into a female shepherd and went about the countryside with the other lasses from the region and took to caring for her own cattle" –even though he comments: "and may it not be thought that because Marcela put herself in that freedom and in such a loose life and with so little or no deliberation, that for that reason has she given indication, not even close, of having her honesty and modesty undermined" (150). But what Marcela really does is exhibit her superior beauty before her admirers who follow her, also dressing themselves as shepherds, among them her victim Grisóstomo, "famous student shepherd", poet and "phoenix of friendship", who dies because of his loves (150).

When they are about to bury him, Ambrosio, who was his friend –notice the two faces– speaks of the kindness of Marcela and says: "She, aside from being cruel, and a little arrogant, and a lot scornful, even envy itself should not nor can it lay any blame". And when he appears, he addresses her: "Oh, fierce basilisk of these mountains!". She demonstrates the point that she is, in fact, arrogant: she does not listen and, on the other hand, demands attention: "And so I beg all of you who are here to be attentive". And she throws herself into defending her attitude and, above all, her "unsolicited" beauty. She says: "And just as the snake does not deserve to be blamed for the poison it possesses and can use to kill, for having been given it by nature, nor do I deserve to be reprimanded for being beautiful; that beauty in the honest woman is like fire set aside or like a sharp sword, that neither burns nor cuts on persons who do not get near. Honor and virtues are adornments of the soul, without which the body, although it might be, ought not to seem beautiful. [...] I was born free and in order to live free I chose the solitude of the countryside. The trees of these mountains are my company, the clear waters of these streams my mirrors" (150–151).

Cervantes does not put the comparison with the snake in Marcela's mouth just because. The serpent, as we know from the Bible, is tempting. And she is allowed to conclude: "May the deceived one complain, may the one who lacked promised hopes despair, may that person I accept be confident, may that person I admire be proud; but let him not call me cruel or homicidal that person whom I do not promise, or deceive, call or accept" (151).

What is the real value of this sentence? Clearly the second part, does not break down this way: "I do not promise, I do not deceive, I do not call, I do not accept". And the imagined shepherd continues: "These mountains have my desires protected, and if from here they leave, it is to contemplate the beauty of the heavens, steps with which the soul travels to its first dwelling". Cervantes concludes: "Without wanting to hear any response, she turned her back and entered into the most secluded section of the mountain that was close by" (151).

Marcela, then, maintains herself safe, defending a freedom that is the shield of that person who disengages from anything that is not her intimate inclination, it is the negation of dialogue, pure Narcissism. For that reason Rosa Chacel, in *Woman in Galleys*, makes the following lucid reflection regarding her: "elusive, unattainable, she remains, and her allegations do not convince anyone. She remains in her absolute symbol: Freedom or Beauty, men will continue to kill themselves for her. Where is the evil?... One must recognize that it is probably in freedom. One should not be frightened: If evil is somewhere, it is in freedom, only in freedom can it be" (151). Without a doubt Cervantes, subtly "disguised", hiding amongst disquisitions about Amadís, Roldán or Dulcinea, in the studied laughter that will provoke the speech of the authentic goat-herders in contrast to the fineness of the false shepherds, and with all of his multicolored literary apparatus, tried to say something to that effect; he wanted, when confronted with a social situation sunk in an overwhelming pretense, but that carried with it a great internal harshness and rigidity, to alert readers to the "disguised" use of the word *freedom.*

Bibliography

Azustre Galiana A., I. Arellao and V. Rocero López, *Demócrito aureo: Los códigos de la risa en el Siglo de Oro (Golden Democritus: The Codes of Laughter in the Golden Age)*, Renacimiento, Sevilla, 2006.

Bosse, M., "El sarao de María de Zayas y Sotomayor: una razón (femenina) de contar el amor (The "sarao" of María de Zayas y Sotomayor: A (Feminine Reason) for Telling Love", CF II.

Cervantes, M. de, *Don Quijote de la Mancha (Don Quixote of the Mancha)*, ed. Martín de Riquer, Planeta, Barcelona, 1980.

Chacel, R., "Artículo II" ("Article II"), *La mujer en galeras* (*Woman in Galleys*), Vol. IV of the *Obras Completas (Complete Works)*, Excma. Diputación of Valladolid, 1993.

Scaramuzza Vidoni, M., *Deseo, imaginación y utopía en Cervantes (Desire, Imagination and Utopia in Cervantes)*, Bulzoni Editors, Rome, 1998.

González González, L. M., *La mujer en el teatro del Siglo de oro español (Woman in the Theater of the Golden Age)*, http: //depace. vah. es.

Hernández Araico, S., "Mudanzas del sarao" ("Movements of the "sarao"), CF II.

Janés, C., *Las primeras poetisas en lengua castellana (The First Women Poets in the Castillian Language)*, Endymión, Madrid, 1986.

Pascual Buxó, J., "Oliva Sabuco de Nantes ("Olivia Sabuco of Nantes"), CF II.

Profeti, M. G., *Quevedo: La scrittura e il corpo (Quevedo: Writing and the Body)*, Bulzoni, Rome, 1984.

Sebastián Castellanos, B., "Del origen de los velos en España" ("About the Origin of Veils in Spain"), El Panorama, Madrid, 1838.

Sepúlveda, J., "Haz y envés de convenciones en El Escondido y la tapada", de Calderón de la Barca ("Pros and Cons of Conventions in The Hidden One and the Covered One", of Calderón de la Barca", *Criticón*, 87-88-89, 2003.

Seseña, N., "Vida en clausura" ("Life in Cloister"), El País, 6th of March, 2007.

VV. AA., *La creatividad femenina en el mundo barroco hispánico. María de Zayas, Isabel Rebeca Correa, Sor Juana Inés de la Cruz (Feminine Creativity in the Hispanic Baroque World. María of Zayas, Isabel Rebeca Correa, Sor Juana Inés de la Cruz)*, I and II, ed. of M. Bosse, B. Potthast and A. Stoll, Kassel, Erfurt, 1999 (Abbreviation: CF).

Yllera, A., "María de Zayas: ¿Una novela de ruptura? Su concepción de la escritura novelesca" ("María of Zayas: A Rupture? Her Conception of Novelistic Writing"), CF I.

VII- Voice of the Quieted Women

When the face of the woman –and her entire body– is hidden behind the *burka* or *marmouk*, it is not a disguise. This dress indicates the negation of the person. She has been converted into a form that moves without being able to salvage the abyss that separates her from the other person through expression and dialogue. Depleted in her freedom, reduced to herself from within what simulates a gag, such is fulfilled that saying of Fray Luis, according to which, and by design of nature, to woman belongs that shutting of her mouth.

Even today, the voices of women that have been stilled are many, voices tied to the earth and its richness and therefore, to the possibility of bearing fruit. Do those voices sleep or, like the earth in winter, await the spring awakening? Or simply achieving the state of full fertility? I can imagine places where writing has not arrived, remote places of Africa or the Amazon jungle... Perhaps those voices are heard fundamentally in the cry, the song of a lullaby or the tearing apart from pain, sickness and death, but also in prayer, the curse and the spell. Those voices are not asleep, no, but they still need to absorb nourishing materials to achieve their fruition. There are, nevertheless, other places that remain silent but that cohabit and with the possibility of bearing fruit, for the whole spectrum of the richness of the earth is latent and in season. They are places where society does not completely overshadow women, but sets them apart, hidden, or at least, differentiated from their masculine counterparts. And thus, while the majority of them might appear lethargic in mutism, some dare to awaken.

Let us leave the West and limit ourselves to areas where this situation provokes enormous contrasts: India, the Arab countries, Iran and Afghanistan. We shall see how these geographic atmospheres bring together backwardness and the greatest refinement; we shall see how in some, as soon as the woman expresses herself, society flowers immediately in social questions, while in others, it is the relationship between the sexes; we shall see how poetry is wrapped in lyricism and humor while prose soon becomes a weapon of denunciation. Given everything, also in these countries and despite the obstacles, wise and firm feminine voices had already arisen in remote antiquity.

INDIAN WISDOM

In India, as deduced from the literature, woman has been writing since antiquity, and even shows off her eloquence without being away from the position she occupies in society. Very soon this fact is reflected in lyric poetry, as in the beautiful anthology *Kuruntokai* (3rd Century B.C. to 3rd Century A.D.)[13], whose poems, of an incomparable beauty and ingenuity, are, in large part, coming from the mouth of a woman, and they usually refer to the lament of

13 See Chapter II, p. 17.

a young woman to a friend because of the separation of her lover who had to leave in search of money to get married, or other peculiar situations, due to the rigidity of the customs around the wedding:

> WHAT SHE SAID:
> (when she was worried because
> he had not hurried to get married)
>
> There is nothing in this place.
> If he is a thief
> and his promises are a lie,
> what will I do?
> Only the heron was here,
> with its young and delicate legs
> like stems of millet,
> observing the lake fish
> in the fugitive current,
> that day when our hearts
> were married. (157)
>
> WHAT SHE SAID:
> (to her friend when he postponed the marriage)
> Friend,
> even though my strength is lost and my virginal beauty
> has faded,
> I am still alive
> in solitude
> like the leaves that bloom during the rains
> among the stubble of the golden millet stems
> and the parrots eat and destroy
> on the hillside fields. (157)

It is not so common to find verses of a similar purity and freshness, even though, as we have seen, there are exceptions. Poems of this type perhaps belonged to oral literature at the beginning. But not all feminine voice from India is manifested as so ingenuous and simple. In the *Mahabhárata*, an epic poem written several centuries before Christ, there is the beautiful story titled "Savitrí", which can be considered a declaration of feminine wisdom. If tree and woman are identified with the Hindu culture in the figure of the *yaḳsis*, the young Savitrí brings together all of the wisdom of the forests. And she who says forest, means road to the mountain-top, crossing the "dark jungle". On this road, the darkness does not frighten her; the jungle, for her, becomes luminous for it is the place of certain threat, of the test and the victory. The threat is the death of her husband Satiaván; the victory, her own word united together with her intelligence.

Savitrí is the other side of Orpheus. If he with his voice dominated the beasts and the trees, she submits to a god. With Satiaván dead, she follows Yama, the god who carries the soul of her husband, and with eloquence she speaks to him of her faith and her mercy. Step by step she enters into lands each time more and more removed from life. For four days the god urges her to withdraw and grants her a gift, but Savitrí continues to approach the fatal place. Finally the god, seduced by her speech, grants her the life of her husband. To each of her eloquent expositions, Yama responds with words like these: "Delight of the heart, stimulus of knowledge, breath of kindness with your words". And at the end he exclaims: "My love for you is growing as you speak. A *joy* for the spirit, a fountain of benefit, your words are a norm of justice. Oh woman devoted to your husband, ask me for incomparable grace!" And thus he enables Satiaván to return to life. Savitrí, then, goes further than Orpheus, perhaps because she lives love like a mercy (158).

India, which has been ahead in almost everything –we need only to mention the discovery of the zero, so important in mathematics– was ahead in creating the image of the intelligent and integrated female. This feminine character is a clear precursor –and transcends– that of Portia, protagonist of *The Merchant of Venice*, of Shakespeare, the wise woman who, thanks to her discourse, saves the life of her husband. And thus, in the Ganges Wars, the feminine voices were able to articulate something, even though, since Antiquity, the situation was harsh: The widow would be burned in the husband's pyre, and the one abandoned by her husband could not have another partner and led a very marginalized life with no rights, conditions that in some way affect women today, even though they live together in emancipation. This allows for the possibility that, together with illiteracy and the lack of any social horizon, there might exist well-known artists, such as Deepa Metha, the poets Sujata Bhatt and Savita Singh, or the novelist Anita Nair. Well aware that the struggle continues today, these artists put forward a committed face.

Savita Singh (1962), with a great literary fineness, appears as an indefatigable warrior. Besides poetry, she writes articles and essays, and teaches political theory at the University of Delhi. Her search for wider horizons is innate in her:

Without Anchor or Tether

The wind would tune an idea
on the head of a bird
that had just finished its nest.
It had come to tell me also
that I am only fruit of the time
and that I am no one to think about my own tran-
scendence.
The sadness that drips ceaselessly within me from a
faucet
rusty and not containable,
is also an opening to a melancholic creation.

Once the afternoon is finished,
the bird being well settled in its place,
leaving me to wander
through the wide world,
without anchor or tether. (159)

With familiarity Savita Singh has recourse to nature, to the birds, the trees, as a transmutation of that very innate Indian feeling from the dawns of its literature, that of the so-named *Aranyakas* ("Books of the Forest"), because she intuits that, through the awareness of man's integration in it, she will arrive at the true freedom. Even the writing seems to be an element that at the same time forms part of the page and the forest:

An Alphabet

I returned, finally,
to the book, of which

I was a page.
I waited until the end
and at the end the trees
said to come.
The jungle called you to the end.

A little bird
at the end, said:
return now
safe, someday someone will come to read you.
For now, continue with alphabets, images, sounds,
there is no one who can decipher you but
the book is the least harmful.
Return to it silently
occupy your space in it
without sound.

Until the end, the same end
I had no desire to do it.
Without success they encouraged me to return.
But of course, I was not myself, after all, an alphabet
in repose for a while
with a yellow page. (160)

Certainly through the poems of Savita Singh the feeling of that atmosphere of the intimate forests reaches us. Not very distant in age, Surekha Vijh (1958) is, like Singh, also interested in politics. Poet, journalist and reporter, who has divided her activities between Washington, London and Delhi, she writes about social and economic themes, without leaving aside the importance of that previous and inevitable step that is the achieving of individual freedom:

Solitude

Do not stay at my side
do not extend your hands to me
let me go alone
and along the sinuous roads
and to look at
the changing moments alone,
precisely alone.

Let me balance
the efficacy of my soul
and the power of the will
to discern among ignorance
and truth
to observe the diverse
shades of light and shadow.

Allow me to know myself
do not stay at my side.
I ought to go on alone. (161)

In this search, in subjective appearance, Surekha Vijh knows well that identity goes joined with the native land, and so she manifests:

India,
I will return to you
to revive my spirit
to elevate my soul
and to breathe the air… (161)

Tear And Smile

But the return is not always easy for someone who has made a definitive life already, and less in our time. And the search and the struggle are not the same from outside or within the country. Retreating briefly in time, we find the voice of Amrita Pritam (1919-2005), the first great writer of the Punjab (Pakistan today), who portrayed the events of the schism of 1947, because of which at least a thousand Muslims, Hindus and Sikhs perished. The verses that follow, that are like a cry, are dedicated to the Sufi Waris Shah:

> You that share aggrieved hearts
> look at your Punjab
> bodies strewn on the ground
> blood flowing in the Chenab. (162)

Amrita Pritam was precocious in her writing in Punjabi language (she published for the first time when she was only 16). After the episodes of 1947, she moved to Delhi and began to write in Hindi, taking in several genres, and she was the first Hindu woman who won important literary prizes like the Sahitya Akademi Award (1956) or the Bhartiya Jnanpith (1982). In the following poem she employs the metaphoric identification of author and verse, giving flight to an image that has roots in the ancient Islamic poetic tradition:

> Encounter
>
> Years later

we found each other by chance
trembling
like a poem…

Night was about to arrive
something was left in the poem
the rest some other place ...

At dawn
we found each other again
like two pieces of paper.
I seized his hand with mine,
he grabbed me by the arm.
We laughed
and with brutal assurance
we censured the poem. (162)

Cultured women, the current Hindu women writers also enjoy the advantage of dominating English along with their own maternal languages, which gives them access, twice over, active and passive, to the universal culture.

Particularly interesting is the vision full of humor of Sujata Bhatt (Ahmedabad, 1956). After living in her native country during her infancy, she studied in the US and presently lives in Germany. In the following poem she appears to smile before some aspects of the Hindu life:

The Virologist
for my father

At 16 he arrived at Benares
to study Ayurvedic medicine.
The first thing he did was to bathe in the Ganges
fulfilling my mother's desires–.

Afterward he felt dirty
and returned to his room
and as he did gave himself another bath.
That afternoon he wrote a letter
to his mother — disappointed
that dipping his foot in the sacred river
had not made him feel more pure.
There had to be something else — there was no doubt.
(163)

Other elements particular to India come and go in her poems, like the serpents, present in numerous verses, behind unexpected lenses:

The Serpent Hunter Speaks

The best way to hunt
Nordic water serpent
is to corner it in a lake and to allow
that it bite you on the arm — it will hold it strongly
maintaining its grip
even if you raise your arm
and you pull it from the water —

Of course, it hurts —
This serpent has a wide head
an enormous jaw, an endowed mouth
and six rows of curved teeth —
And it will defend itself —

But then you have it —
There are ways
to calm it.
After all, it is not a poisonous
northern water snake —

It is timid, elusive
and only attacks
when confronted.

Then after,
I always let it go —
When my students have already looked at it,
they have observed it watching it fixedly for months,
taking notes.

I release it in the forests.
It is so quick, a sudden lightning bolt
of energy, a black spark
rushing like a black arrow out of my hands. (164)

The Lyre Lurking In Wait For The Arab Woman

To what extent modernity and tradition, struggle and smile cohabit in India and in the work of these writers is notable, just as notable as their multicolored world. Let us take a step now toward the East and we shall see how in the Arab countries something similar happens, but with different shades, and how sex occupies an important place and the women's struggle is carried out directly through prose. It is also true that in these countries women had been writing since antiquity, since the first period of Islam, but they would do it, above all, either the princesses or the party cheerleaders –parties for men–, wine pourers or singers, like some of the Arab-Andalusian women. The freedom with which they expressed themselves leaves us helpless before what is happening today, and it is hard for us to believe that, within the Arab world, there appear the differences that do, and that, together with the women poets who have made a mark, true highlights even of the modernization of literature, there exists an immense majority of women hidden and almost mute.

Two names dominate in the Arabic lyric of the 20th Century, the Palestinian Fadwa Tuqán and the Iraqi woman Nazik Al-Malaika. Al-Malaika (1923-2007) was the driver behind the Free Verse movement, along with Badr Shakir al-Sayyab. Knowledgeable about universal literature, with mastery, in her verses there are echoes of both Shakespeare and Shelley, and with the same mastery she undertakes the defense of the rights of women in search of their identity:

> I
> Night asks itself who am I.
> I am its deep secret, restless
> and black, its rebel secret.
> I have hidden my essence in silence.
> I have wrapped my essence in silence,
> and I have remained here, pallid, inert,
> seeing how the centuries ask
> who am I.
> The wind asks itself who am I.
> I am its surprising breath, renegade of time,
> and, the same as it, I do not have a place.
> We keep on walking without end,
> passing eternally, and upon arriving at the summit,
> we find only the end of misery;
> and then, nothingness.
> The time asks who am I.
> As he, a proud one who devours the eras,

and endows them with life again.
I believe the far–off past,
of an easy, seductive hope,
so that I myself can return to bury it.
And then be able to forge myself a different past,
and a frozen tomorrow.

The essence asks itself who am I.
Like it, I walk firm in the mists,
without anything that peace provides for me.

I keep on asking, and the answer
continues being also a mirage.
And even though I believe it to be nearby –as always–
upon arriving at its side, it has vanished.
It disappears. It dies. (165-166)

As for the Palestinian Fadwa Tuqán, born in Nablús in 1917, she writes the chronicle of the suffering of a people occupied by Israel through her poems. Indefatigable in the struggle, she died in December 2003, during the Intifada. From a very young age she found herself pained by history, incubating a voice that would rise up as profound and piercing:

ALWAYS ALIVE
Dear country, no.
In spite of everything that revolves, in the somber steppes,
around you, the stone of pain.
They will not be able, my love,
to tear out your eyes.
They will not be able.

May they strangle the dreams, the hope!

May they nail on the cross
the freedom to construct and to work!
May they rob the children's laughter!
Let them burn!
Let them destroy…!
From the same misery.
From our great misery.
From the blood spilled on our walls.
[…]
From the tremor of life and death,
Life will arise in you again.
You, old wound of ours!
Our sorrow!
Our only love! (167)

The Sustained Struggle Of Prose

This creative height cohabits with the most terrible social backwardness in all respects. The progressive growth of rigorous Islam in countries like Egypt, where in 10 years numbers of covered women have increased from 10% to 90%, gives us much to think about. This is joined together with social paralysis. It is logical that in these places some women speak for those who cannot speak, and thus we have outstanding examples in the prose writers, who say what they need to say, such as Fátima Mernissi in Morocco, Assia Djebar in Algiers or Nawal Al-Sa'dawi in Egypt.

Fátima Mernissi is the author of numerous books, but it would have been enough for her to have written *Morocco through its Women* to occupy the position she does in this respect. Historian and sociologist, she considers that the problem of the situation of the female in Morocco is more political than religious, and in the aforementioned book she responds, through a series of interviews, to these questions: What woman hides behind the veil? How does she, who has abandoned the tradition of her ancestors, live and dare to show her face? That which is gathered in her pages, she says, derives from the "capturing of the real". And the real, in this case, is the silencing by way of ignorance and religious coercion, and it is so brutal that it is startling.

The problems which the interviewed women have had to confront since they were little girls (many have begun to work at the age of five or six, torn from their families and their native land), revolve around two main points: one related to sex and the other to the outside world. And they range from the struggle to free oneself from a marriage imposed during infancy to the need for work, as degrading as the conditions might be, to combat misery.

Regarding the relationship of these women with the man, the social position occupies a very important place, since it situates them in a different way before masculine abuse. Thus, for example, a woman named Merien confesses: "I began to ask about the ways to abort and he applied all of them to me, one by one. One of the first ones consisted of drinking the juice of six lemons with a tablespoon of strong pepper". Other evidence that is translated in the pages of Fátima Mermissi is the eagerness that young Moroccan men have to learn, to free themselves from family dependency (168).

More interesting, literarily, are the works of the Algerian

Assia Djebar and the Egyptian Nawal Al-Sa'dawi. The former –of French education– is the author of intelligent novels where the condition of woman is always reflected as well as the historical situation of her country. Let us look at two of them: *Love, the Fantasy*, and *Sultan Shadow*. Both are founded on a duality, the former because of interposition of time periods of the episodes relayed: a historical event and a current one are mixed; the latter, *Sultan Shadow*, for dealing with two feminine characters who live together and represent two states of cultural evolution.

Assia Djebar, who is also a filmmaker, in her writing unfolds events before our eyes as if the page were a screen, in such a way that they move in a kaleidoscope. Thus in *Love, the Fantasy*, one sees concrete images of a dead tribe –massacred– in the caves of El Kantara in 1830, the guerrilla from a century later, the lover of Benkadruma, exposed as an idol, covered in jewels, the cathartic dance of a grandmother, the gesture of a woman who warms the foot of a girl with each hand, while in *Sultan Shadow* that shadow captivates us, that dark woman who collects herself in the cavern where all the echoes are nourished and which is the depository of ancestral life: she attends to the little children always hanging off her skirts, she does not know more than submission or punishment and she is always covered. The other, on the other hand, the emancipated one, the Sultan, enjoys, makes love and develops a multicolored dance full of reflections with her life, even though in final analysis these turn out to be mirages.

Assia Djebar obtained the Peace Prize from the Frankfurt Fair in 2002. In *Sultan Shadow*, she narrates the first matrimonial relationship:

> Rape? Is it this? People say it's your husband, your mother says: "Your master, your lord" ... Fights in the bed, discovering for yourself an unknown vigor. His chest smashes you. You slide away, you try to escape his weight, you become increasingly more rigid –arms spastically clutched against your ribs– inside the embrace. [...] You close your eyes, the end is near, and you renew the resistance. [...] The moment when you will have submerged yourself comes closer. Close yourself off: eyes, ears and the bottom of your heart. Allow yourself to capsize!
>
> "Don't be afraid, little one!" – he peels off incomprehensible words.
> Is it necessary to give in? No, remember the streets, they extend themselves in you beneath a sun that has dispersed the clouds [....] you see the outside space again where you navigate every day. When the man's phallus tears into you, rapid sword, you cry out in the silence, in your silence: "No ... no!" You fight, he beats up on you, you try to come up to the surface. "Let yourself go", whispers the voice in your temple.
> The phallus continues, and the burn comes alive in the darkness that is progressively killing in you the images of defense. You don't perceive anything more than a gurgle. The male has pulled himself apart, and your legs hang [...] The man has disappeared into the bathroom. When he returns, he throws a towel at you, that lies on top of your stained legs.
> Look at my legs! And look at my blood! He has bought that right! ... (169)

But perhaps of these three prose writers, the most politically committed and the most persecuted is Nawal Al Sa'dawi (1931). A doctor as a profession, author of more than 30 books, student of the problems of the female from all points of view, she introduced herself as a writer with *The Hidden Face of the Arab Woman*, where she exposed all of the cases that, as a psychiatrist and rural doctor, she had had to attend to, finding seriously weak situations, among other things, and ritual poisonings, abortions or clitoris ablations. She fought against poverty, discrimination, was jailed, lived in exile, was subject to trial for apostasy, and she has not stopped referencing and calling attention to injustice, pain and suffering lived by her contemporaries in Islamic countries, with a lucidity that causes her to highlight, as Fátima Mernissi did, the political roots of this situation, above the religious ones. That "Concepción Arenal of the Islamic world", as Fanny Rubio said of her once, utilizes science as a method of knowing the feminine identity.

In 1991 she visited Madrid and we were able to see her and to listen to her testimony. She proceeded to become the General Director of Health in Egypt, her country, although she was ultimately fired and jailed by Anwar El-Sadat. She was also director of the Association of Solidarity of the Arab Woman, of a consulting nature for the United Nations. In addition, she is a great writer, as the novels *Women at Point Zero* and *The Fall of the Faith* demonstrate. Her Arabic roots, fertilized by universal culture, offer up an unexpected fruit, that in her hands is transformed into true mastery. In *Woman at Point Zero*, the real and terrible story of a prostitute who was executed for killing her pimp, narrated with a chilling efficiency, she leaves testimony of the last interviews held with her and of all the miseries lived by this woman and that provoked her to that sole action undertaken to free herself from an unsustainable situation. Along with *Woman at Point Zero* –and other works–, *The Fall of the Faith* appears to be a complex novel, autogenic, of a high literary level, disconcerting and seductive at the same time, in which the theme of Islam, and the situation of man and woman in society, are going to end up in another great theme –that of freedom. Eastern because of its colorful mix and Western because of its modernity, it is a master work of the contemporary Arab narrative.

But I will not detain myself in reviewing all of the novels of Nawal Al Sa'dawi, but limit myself to quoting a brief fragment from *The Hidden Face of the Arab Woman*, an interview where the topic is ablation of the clitoris. Referring to the women questioned, the truly silenced ones, the author observes:

> [...] the majority of them did not have the least idea of the harm that had been inflicted on them with the cleavage, and, in addition, some of them thought it was good for their health, that it cleansed and "purified" them.
> The interviews in general develop in this manner:
> —How old were you then?
> —I was still a girl. I must have been seven or eight.
> —Do you remember the operation with any detail?
> —Of course, how could I forget it?
> —Were you afraid?
> —A lot. I hid in the top of the closet (in other cases they say under the bed or in the neighbors' house), but they caught me and my whole body trembled in their arms.

> —Did it hurt?
> —A lot. It was as if they were burning me. I screamed with all my strength. My mother held down my head so that I could not move it, my aunt the right arm and my grandmother took care of the left. Two women, whom I had never seen, kept me from moving my legs and forcefully separated them. The "daya" sat between those two women, with a sharp razor in her hand, and with it she cut off my clitoris. I was terrified and the pain that burned me up was so intense that I lost consciousness.
> —What happened after the operation?
> —Everything hurt me, and I was in bed for several days before I could even move. The wound continued bleeding for quite a while, and my mother changed my clothing twice a day.
> —When you discovered that they had removed a little organ from your body, how did you feel?
> —They told me that if it wasn't done to a girl, people would talk about her, she would not behave well, and when she got to marrying age, she would begin to run after men, without any of them wanting her as a wife.
> [....]
> —Did you believe what they told you?
> —Of course. The day I recovered from the operation I was very happy, I felt that I had freed myself from something bad, I felt clean and pure. (171–172)

A few years ago, the accusation of apostasy that weighed over Nawal Al Sa'dawi was finally suspended, one that would have left her at 71 almost defenseless, running the risk of being expelled from Islam and at the mercy of those fanatics who would have had license to kill her. Presently, the writer continues her fight in El Cairo, but she can rarely be mentioned in public. For me it seems that I see her, with her vigorous white hair and her enormous sense of humor. A woman not covered up, a woman who presents an entire face and all of her interior world as a missile.

The Tribal Song Of The Body

Let us return to poetry, taking a step toward the East, and let us note the symbolic value of the lyric that, without the need to be as direct as prose, can also be converted into a weapon. Let us stay with Iran and concentrate on a single woman, a great revolutionary including in everything having to do with literary style. Nor was Forugh Farrojzad (1935-1967) veiled, the first contemporary Persian woman poet, who suffered the evolution of her country in reverse. That is, she was born in a time of opening up, in the times of Reza Shah, who attempted to modernize things, constructed railroads, created schools with co-education, imposed the abolition of the chador by force –if on the other hand he imprisoned those he considered his enemies, among them many intellectuals, in prison ... Given everything, in middle class families tradition was followed, and the same for Forugh, whose father was a professional military man, although with her sister Purán she frequented a co-educational elementary school, suffered from the iron-clad paternal authority and from the obsolete travel concepts of a society anchored in the past. She was still a child when Reza Shah was deposed, after the occupation of the country by English and Russian troops. At that time, she liked children's stories and sleeping on the roof of her house during the summer. At 13 she already wrote poetry in classical meters. At 15 she studied painting. During that same period she fell in love with a distant relative 15 years older than she, and obtained permission to marry. She then had the child who would be her only child, Kamyar, and began to take part in literary life. For her free and singular character, she immediately suffered harassment from men, and at the same time, the rejection then from that exclusively masculine atmosphere.

After her marriage, Forough Farrojzad begins to publish and her voice makes clear all of her emotional spectrum: she ranges from a lullaby for the little one who "bothers her mother", to the "sin" that awakens her regret. She is 18 when her first book *Captive* appears, whose iconoclastic poems were free in all concepts, especially those related to the behavior of women, and which the academics did not approve. It turns out to be so scandalous that the religious authorities arrest the owner of the largest bookstore in Iran for having published it. This has to do with verses that radiate vitality, amorous despair, joy, reproaches, solitude, abandon, doubt, dreams ... in these man is proud, possessive, unfaithful, conqueror ... Forugh feels herself distant from conventional roles assigned to women. Her marriage is on the verge of collapsing. She divorces, but the child remains in the custody of the husband, who will never consent that he have any contact with the mother again; this will be a wound from which she will not be able to stabilize herself, and they say that, in an unspoken way, carried her to her death. The poet tries to to return to her family home but is thrown out by her father. During her absence, "The Bilitis of Iran" is published, an article where ironic poems about the "sins" that she confesses are cited.

The disapproval intensifies, the rumors scandalize men and women. In 1959 Forugh leaves for England to study film production and in 1962 produces a film about the colony of lepers in Tabriz, *The House is Black*, for which they grant her the prize for the best documentary. During these years, a rebirth of the arts and poetry takes place in Teheran, and she is its pivotal figure. In 1964, she publishes another book, *New Birth*, that critics point out as an important marker in modern Persian poetry. In February of 1967 she was preparing to interpret the role of the protagonist of Bernard Shaw's Saint Joan when, after visiting her mother, driving home and overwhelmed by malaise, to avoid an oncoming vehicle at a crossroads, she threw herself against a wall and died.

Forugh Farrojzad was too disturbing for the intellectuals, including those of Iran prior to the Ayatolas. It had to do with a new style, in her life as well as in her writing. Forugh writes the poem of conversation, of everyday language, and, with the same naturalness, adapts traditional quantitative meters and, curiously, expresses the conflict between man and woman in the manner of a conflict in style.

"My entire existence is a dark verse", so begins *New Birth*. For the poem, in fact, it is a moving toward the light, toward the "dawn of the eternal growth". Her death moved all of Iran and rumors were spread that she had crashed deliberately. Her poem, "Let's have faith in the beginning of the cold season" seemed to predict it. It was also said then that, among the great poets of contemporary Iran, only she could be compared with the great Nima. It was also said that after Hafez Shirazi, she was the greatest Persian poet of all time.

One of her poems that in their day constituted a great scandal, although from our contemporary perspective we cannot detect the novelty that it supposed, is the one titled:

BORDER WALLS
Now once more in the silenced night
as plants grow
walls of closure, frontier walls,
to guard over the fields of love.

Now again more rumors from the city
like murky schools of frightened fish
emigrate from my dark shore.
Now once more the windows
open to the joyful contact of spread out perfumes
now the trees, asleep in the garden, undress from their
bark
and the earth, through a thousand pores,
absorbs confused particles of moonlight.

Now
come closer
and listen
the obsessive heartbeats of love
that spread
like the "tom tom" of the black drums
in the tribal song of my body.

I feel
I know
what is the instant of prayer
now all the stars
lie together in sleep.

I, through the refuge of the night
from the end of every breeze I run
in the refuge of the night
crazed I collapse
with my heavy hair in your hands
and I regale you with tropical flowers from this green
and warm zone.

Come with me
come with me to that star
not to the star that is a thousand years away
from the distance of the weight of the earth and the
deception of its forms
where nobody
is afraid of the light.
I in the islands that float in the water breathe
I
in the immense sky seek out a fragment
that may be free from empty thoughts.

Return with me
return with me
to the beginning of my body
to the perfumed center of the fetus
to the instant when I was created from you
return with me
from you I am incomplete.

Now the doves
fly above the peaks of my breasts
now in the buds of my lips
the butterflies of kisses have sunk ready to flee
now the mihrab
of my body
is ready for the prayer of love.

Return with me
I am incapable of speaking
because I love you
because "I love you" is a word
that comes from the world of the vain
and from the old and reiterated
return with me
I am incapable of speaking.

Let me deposit the burden of light in the refuge of the night
let it fill me up
with small drops of rain
of tender hearts
of forms of unborn children
let it fill me up
perhaps my love
may be the cradle for the new Messiah that is about to be born. (175-176)

Under The Burka

And let us move from these women not only uncovered –Forugh died still in the time of the Shah, before the rise to power of the Ayatollah Khomeini–, but they show their face and say what they have to say at the risk of their life, to the most covered up, the most silenced, the Afghan women, those whose body remains completely hidden –including the eyes– under the *burka,* but in spite of that, have expressed themselves in brief poems impressive for their beauty and their strength and for the inner freedom that they reflect, even though we refer here to poems mostly anonymous and not written.

Years ago, the Afghan women could sing when going for water to the fountain and at the festive gatherings, while the man of their land devoted himself exclusively to the preparations for war. This minimal freedom was cut short by the arrival of the Taliban, but secretly they kept on singing. Even though, as I have said, underneath the *burka* and living in the harshest of conditions, being, in general, illiterate, these women have polarized in their society the art of poetry through some brief poems called *landay*. They are unwritten verses and lack models and poetic authorities, but they preserve the force of emblematic echoes of the people. They are simple and essential, sons and daughters of terrestrial beings that celebrate nature, forests, rivers, the hours of the day and they nourish themselves on war, honor, kindness, love and death; anonymous fruit in permanent emulation, cries from the heart, sparkling like lightning.

These poems were collected by an Afghan writer, Said Bahodine Mahruj, in the book titled *Suicide and Song*, perhaps triggering the censure toward him which cost him his life. On speaking of the theme, I base myself fundamentally on this work which I myself translated into Castillian.

Said Bahodine Mahruj, born February 12, 1928, Pakistan –was a doctor of Philosophy from the University of Montpellier, Dean of the School of Letters of Kabul and governor of the province of Kapica and, fundamentally, a poet. After the Soviet invasion of Afghanistan, he exiled himself to Peshawar where he founded the Afghan Center of Information. As I noted, one of the reasons for which he was assassinated, which happened February 11, 1988, in Peshawar, was the interest in the question of women in his country, and not only did he collect their songs but he also denounced the brutal life to which they were subjected and their absolute defenselessness, since for the least mistake they could be stoned.

Forming part of a warrior community *par excellence*, the Afghans who speak Pashtun should subject themselves to the rules established by masculine values and to their brutal honor code. They submit, in fact, but they do not accept, such that in their songs they allow their rebel and proud face to be seen:

> In secret I burn, in secret I cry,
> I am the Pashtun woman who cannot reveal her love.
> (178)

In this community, the woman takes care of the fields and the herd, the flour, of baking the bread, spinning, sewing, putting the animal furs out to dry, transporting the water, or whatever might be necessary, in heavy jugs that she carries on her head. In exchange, she never complains, rarely mentions her "velvet fingers" with which she gathers ears of grain or the pressure of the jug that her back barely supports. She suffers above all the moral aspect of her servitude. Welcomed with sadness from the cradle –the father takes as grief the birth of a girl who will only be a coin of exchange between the clan families without her ever being consulted–, she is humiliated to the point that not even her husband lowers himself to eat with her. Given everything, endowed with a special temple of cheer, the Afghan woman seems to despise these gestures and only laments the negation of love:

> Oh, my God! You send me again the dark night.
> And again I tremble from head to feet, for I have to enter
> the bed I hate.
>
> Crude people, you see that an old man is dragging me toward his bed.
> And you ask why I cry and tear out my hair! (178)

The Pashtun woman suffers the extreme consequences of the rules of society, even when it had to do with their children. She is the one who sends her son off to a war of "vendetta", the one who advises him to behave like a hero, to run the risk of not returning alive –and if he returns injured, he should display his wounds on his chest and not on the back–. On the other hand, he who sees her when she finds out about the death of her son in the field of honor, he has the impression of finding himself before a person free from all maternal "weakness". It is because that lad, whom she calls "son", is for her a man who already belongs to the masculine community. There are well-founded reasons that explain such an exceptional reaction: from the work of a slave that she is carrying out, the heaviest and hardest part is related to the considerable number of children that she should feed and educate. And she sees more than half of them die at different ages: that spectacle can harden the heart.

The Son And The Horrible Little One

The son, barely an adolescent, begins to beat his mother. Their cries of brutality and cruelty on their mother constitute a form of initiation to adult life, a proof of strength. And the father attends these scenes of affirmation of the son with an accommodating indifference. On the other hand, the sons are generally fruit of a forced matrimony, doubles of a husband who behaves as an absolute and tyrannical master.

Among these imposed husbands, cruel and lazy, who live their image of hypothetical hero fatuously, and who treat their wives like animals, and those sons encouraged to follow the same model, the Afghan woman, apparently submissive, carries out a revolution that ends up in two testimonies: suicide and song. Given that suicide, according to the Pashtun code, is a cowardice, and that Islam forbids it, a man would never commit it. The woman, upon realizing that, tragically proclaims her rejection of the community law. In the same way, with her song she carries out a challenge of a similar nature that can be revealed as fatal for the themes she treats and one fundamentally: love for the lover.

> Lover of mine come to satiate
> the sorrel of my heart which has broken all of its bridles.

> Your love is water, it is fire.
> Flames consume me, waves swallow me. (180)

In the Afghan community, woman's love is a serious mistake punished by death. The undisciplined women are killed coldly. Massacres of the women lovers carry an interminable tale of clan revenge. But the women do not renounce the secret love –that represents freedom–, on the other hand, not a single couplet speaks of conjugal love. Fidelity is reserved only for the male lover. Thus her verses are perpetual cries of separation, and the imposed husband –generally an old man or a child– is called "the little horrible one" and frequently treated as a joke.

> The "horrible little one" does not do anything: not love or war.
> At night as soon as he has his belly full, he goes up to bed and
> snores until dawn.
>
> Oh, lord. The long and sad night is here again.
> And he is here again, my "horrible little one", and he sleeps…
>
> Open a hole in the wall and kiss my mouth,
> The "horrible little one" is a builder and will know how to fix it. (180)
>
> The lover, as we have seen, inspires in her other accents:
> My lover wants me to embrace him among the branches of the apple tree,
> and I climb from branch to branch to give him my mouth.

> Put your mouth on mine,
> but leave my tongue free to so that I can speak to you of love.
>
> At your side I am beautiful, my mouth stretched out,
> my arms open.
> And you, like a coward, let yourself rock by sleep.
>
> Take me first between your arms, hold me,
> only later will you be able to tie yourself to my velvet muscles.
>
> Learn to eat my mouth!
> Arrange your lips, and then sweetly force the
> line of my lips. (180-181)

To Die Under The Knife Blows

The woman, passionate, as we see, invites the man to love, not with tenderness, but instead harassing him in his dignity, with a juice of audacity, and citing the courageous warrior to run risks:

> Give me your hand, oh my love, and let us leave for the fields
> to love each other or to fall victim together to the knifeblows. (181)

These accents, in the game of love, are true provocations. But, what do they represent, in reality, the verses when compared to the codes of virile society? Frequently a burst of laughter. Through them, their women authors escape the man that sees them as property, carrying their own attitude to extreme consequences, obliging him –including the son– to behave like a hero, for otherwise he will become the object of a bloody derision. That is, by means of the verse, the Afghan woman lays a trap for man by resorting to her own values:

> Love of mine, go first to avenge the blood of the martyrs,
> before deserving the refuge of my breasts.
>
> Return riddled with the bullets of a dark weapon, oh love,
> I will sew your wounds and give you my mouth. (181)

Other times it has to do simply with an ironic declaration:

> Oh love of mine, if in my arms you tremble so much
> what will you do when the clashing of swords
> becomes a thousand lightning bolts? (182)

Constantly in contact with death, the Pashtun woman conceives this final moment in a particular way. In her vocabulary, there is no trace of the word "soul" or "ruh", she uses the word "sa", that means breathing. She talks about "the end of breathing", for what she sings is exclusively the destiny of the body, exalting an element of this physical reality: the heart, seat of all emotions, which she compares to a bird, a fountain of blood, an oven that devours its own flames. She speaks, then, of the geography of her body; its fragile growth, its grains of beauty like stars, its breasts like grenades. And together with this, of death, that for these essential singers, daughters of the earth, it is a return to the elements: dust, wind, grass, water, fire. And naturally, they speak to us also of the ephemeral character of their existence:

> Rapid love of mine, I want to offer you my mouth,
> Death hovers around the town and wants to carry me off.
>
> My beautiful lover, they will kill you someday,
> do not offer me flowers now in the middle of the road. (182)

Enemy Bullets

Everything said up until now reveals the face of the Pashtun woman until April of 1978. A change was produced with the Communist *coup d'état*, and then the Soviet invasion that razed the country, with the accompanying jailings, tortures, summary executions, destruction of towns, burnings of harvest and massacres, like that of Kerala, where after an attack from resisters, all of the men were killed (1, 700). The only survivors, women and children, moved on to occupy a refugee camp in Pakistan.

After the invasion by the Red Army, December 27, 1979, the great manifestation of April, 1980, was carried out by women. Girls from the schools and institutes of Kabul, college students, teachers, employees, and mothers of families went to the Government Palace. Russian tanks intervened. Nahid, one of the organizers of the march, questioned the official, a member of the Afghan Communist Party, who was pointing a gun at her, almost with a couplet: "Hey, little coward! Since you are incapable of defending the honor of your country, you are not a man. Take my veil, put it on your head and give me your weapon (183)". The official fired and Nahid collapsed lifeless. Those massacres and deportations (three million people from the interior moved to the neighboring country) did not do away with poetic creation, which survived in the fields. The nostalgia of the earth and combat then passed to the foreground.

> —Breeze that you blow from the other side of the mountains where
> my beloved fights.
> What message do you bring me?
> —The message of that distant lover is the smell of cannon dust
> and this dust of the ruins that arrives with me.
>
> It is spring, here the leaves grow on the branches,
> but in my country the leaves have lost their branches
> under the dew of enemy bullets.
>
> Go fight in Kabul, love of mine,
> for you I will preserve intact my body and mouth. (183)

The Triumph Of Love

What is happening in the present day? Neither did that terrible law that the Taliban imposed do away with those profound, angry voices, and surely it accentuated them since they were totally hidden. It is very probable that now, since they can be seen through the window slits –although one must not have illusions– their voices crying for what truly is important to them can again be heard: their autonomy when it comes to love, because that force of love can only end up triumphing, that is, sprouting incessantly with intensity, for it is what moves life itself. Their victory, like the couplets, will always be above religions and fanatics. Without a doubt these women, most of them still underneath the *burka*, intuit that in the violent and anguished world that is ours to live, this is the only weapon that is at the reach of everyone:

> Come and be a flower in my chest
> so that I can refresh you each morning with a burst of laughter.
>
> If you did not know how to love,
> why have you awakened my sleeping heart?
>
> My mouth belongs to you, devour it, do not fear anything.
> It is not sugar, it does not run the risk of melting.
>
> My love, open my tomb and contemplate
> the dusk that covers the beautiful intoxication of my eyes. (184)

Bibliography

Al Saddawi, N., *La caída del Imán* (*The Fall of the Iman*), Sexi Barral, Barecelona, 1995.

__________. *Mujer en punto cero* (*Woman at Point Zero*), Horas y horas, Madrid, 1994.

__________. *La cara desnuda de la mujer árabe (The Naked Face of the Arab Woman)*, Horas y Horas, Madrid, 1991.

Bahodine Mahruh, S., *El suicidio y el canto* (*Suicide and Song*), Ediciones del Oriente y del Mediterráneo, Guadarrama, 2002.

Bhatt, S., *Augatora* (*Augatora*), Ediciones del Oriente y del Mediterráneo, Guadarrama, 2003.

Djebar, A., *El amor y la fantasía* (*Love and Fantasy*), Ediciones del Oriente y del Mediterráneo, Guadarrama, 1990.

__________. *Sombra sultana* (*Sultan Shadow*), Ediciones del Oriente y del Mediterráneo, Guadarrama, 1995.

Farrojzad, F., *Nuevo nacimiento* (*New Birth*), Ediciones del Oriente y del Mediterráneo, Guadarrama, 2003.

Kuruntokai (*Kuruntokai*), Ed. Dr. M. Shumugam Pillari, Koodal Publishers, Madruai, 1976.

Martínez Montávez, P., *El poema es filistín (Palestina en la poesía árabe actual) (The Poem es Philistine (Palestine in Contemporary Arabic Poetry)*, Molinos de Agua, Madrid, 1980.

Mernissi, F., *Marruecos a través de sus mujeres (Morocco Through its Women)*, Ediciones del Oriente y del Mediterráneo, 1990.

Prasad Ganguly, S. y A. Villaverde, *India: Poesía contemporánea* (*India: Contemporary Poetry*), Ediciones Libertarias y World Difusion, Madrid, 1994.

Quince siglos de poesía árabe (*antología*) (*15 Centuries of Arabic Poetry* (*Anthology*), trans. of Martínez Montávez, Reivsta Lateral, Torremolinos, 1998.

Singh, S., en *Las voces del árbol* (in *The Voices in the Tree*), http: //www. adamar. org.

Savitrí, *Un episodio del Mahabhárata* (*An Episode of the Mahabhárata*), Ediciones del Oriente y del Mediterráneo, Guadarrama, 1998.

Vijh, S., *Until the Next Harvest*, A Writers Workshop Redbird, Calcutta, 1987.

www.ingramcontent.com/pod-product-compliance
Lightning Source LLC
LaVergne TN
LVHW091046080826
845145LV00002B/638

* 9 7 8 1 9 4 9 9 3 8 0 7 4 *